Sampler Book 6, Ontario in Colour Photos, Saving Our History One Photo at a Time

Photography by Barbara Raué ©2018

Series Name: Cruising Ontario

Sampling from several towns

Each photo I take that precedes a demolition, or a natural disaster such as a tornado or a fire, is meeting this aim of mine of Saving Our History One Photo at a Time. There are more than 100 towns already photographed which you can visit without moving from a comfortable chair in your living room. ©All the photos in this book have been taken with my cameras. I own the rights to them. I confirm that I will never submit any content for which I do not have the exclusive publishing rights. I will adhere to all terms in the Content Guidelines when publishing new content.

Cover: 83 Fox Street, Penetanguishene, Page 61

Table of Contents

Welland, Ontario – My Top 13 Picks

Kingston, Ontario – My Top 23 Picks

Ottawa, Ontario – My Top 11 Picks

Midland, Ontario – My Top 15 Picks

Penetanguishene, Ontario – My Top 9 Picks

Kemptville, Ontario and Area – My Top 6 Picks

Cornwall, Ontario – My Top 9 Picks

Welland, Ontario – My Top 13 Picks

Welland is located in the centre of Niagara. Within a half-hour, residents can travel to Niagara Falls, Niagara-on-the-Lake, St. Catharines, Port Colborne or Buffalo. It has been traditionally known as the place *where rails and water meet*, referring to the railways from Buffalo to Toronto and Southwestern Ontario, and the waterways of the Welland Canal and Welland River, which played a great role in the city's development. The city is separated by the Welland River and Welland Canal which links Lake Erie and Lake Ontario.

The city was first settled in 1788 by United Empire Loyalists. Welland, because of its proximity to the Sir Adam Beck hydroelectric station at Niagara Falls, was historically known for its steel, automotive, and textile industries. Manufacturing firms were the biggest employers in Welland, with companies like Union Carbide, United Steel, Plymouth Cordage Company, three drop forges, a cotton mill, and the Atlas Steel Company, as well as general manufacturing plants, influencing the shaping of early Welland.

The Plymouth Cordage Company was the first major industrial company to open a plant in Welland in 1906. It was a rope making company with headquarters in Plymouth, Massachusetts; it became the largest manufacturer of rope and twine in the world. Plymouth binder twine was popular among farmers to package farm crops such as grass, wheat and straw, and was the inspiration for the naming of the Plymouth brand of automobiles first produced in 1928 Many workers who relocated to Welland from the company's operations in Plymouth were of Italian origin. To minimize the potential effects of cultural and language barriers, Plymouth Cordage sent four foremen to Welland: one was Italian, one was French, one was German and one was English.

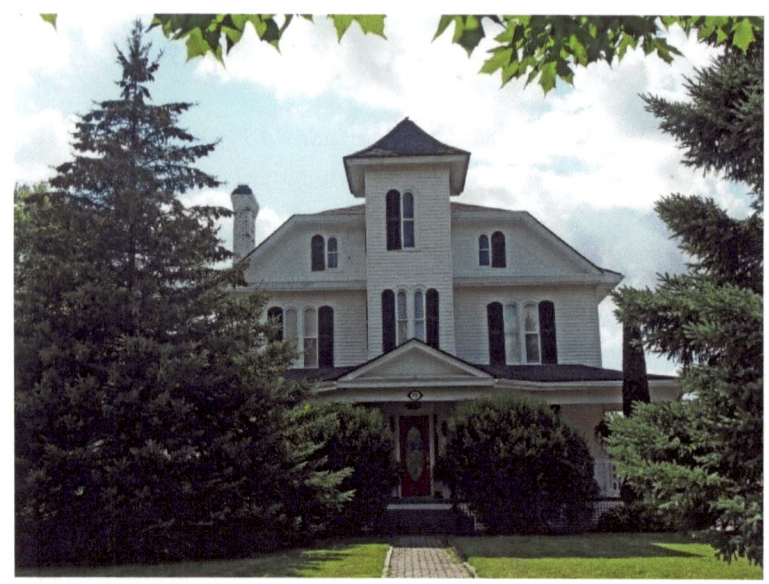

131 Aqueduct Street – Bagar-Bison House – 1880 – Victorian - Two-storey tower, pediment, fish scale pattern on upper storey, sidelights around door – Welland Book 1

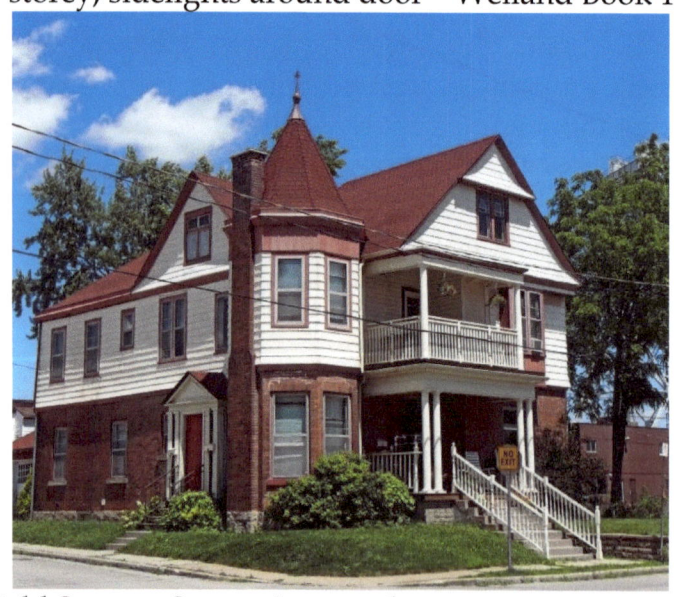

30 Bald Street – Queen Anne style, two-storey turret with cone-shaped cap, second floor sleeping porch

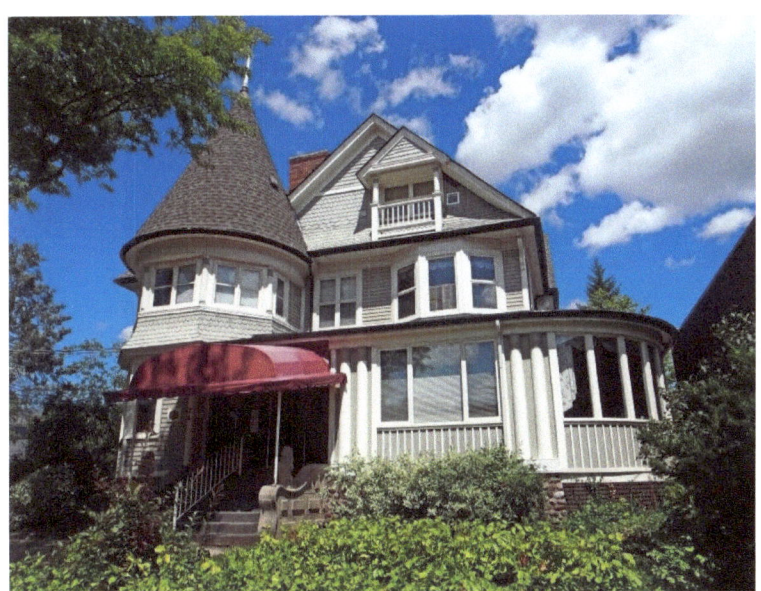

24 Burgar Street – The Glasgow-Fortner House – 1859 – Queen Anne style – now Rinderlins Dining Rooms

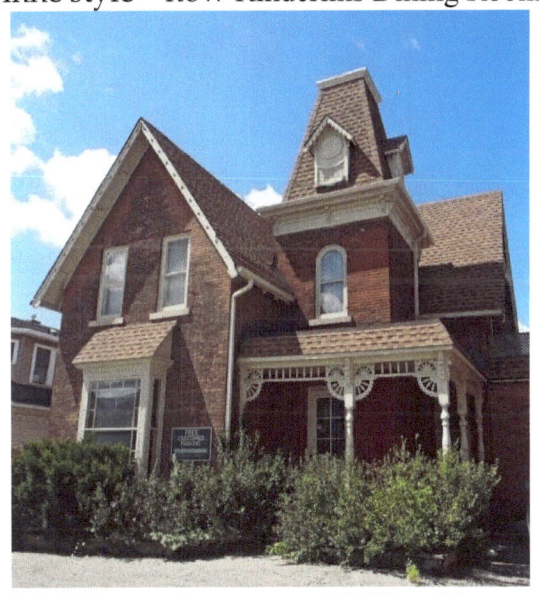

204 East Main Street – Lawrence-Phillips House – c. 1890 – Victorian style with a mixture of Gothic, Tuscan Italianate and Queen Anne elements

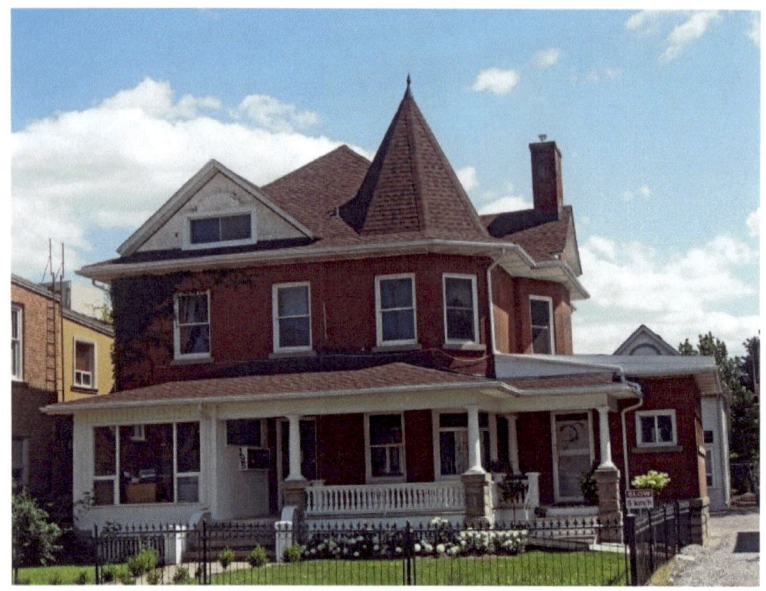
195 East Main Street – Victorian style

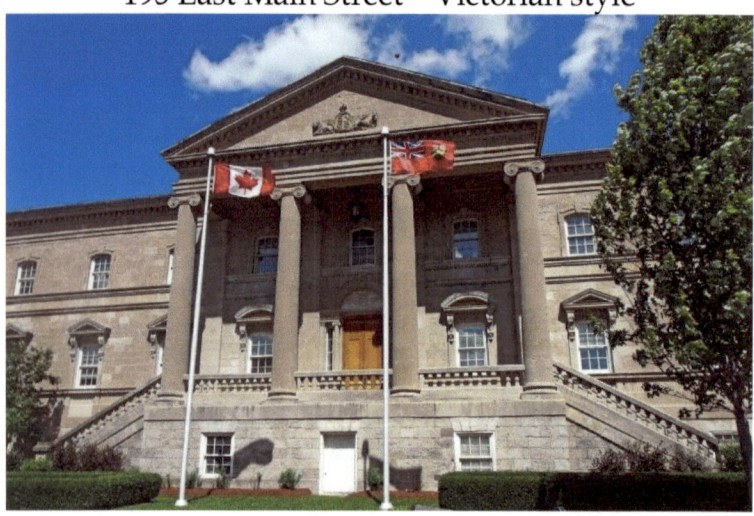
102 East Main Street - Welland County Court House – built in 1855-56, four years after the creation of Welland County; Neo-Classical style, built of Queenston limestone – the front of the building is dominated by a huge projecting portico surmounted by a classical pediment and four large Ionic columns, sidelights beside door

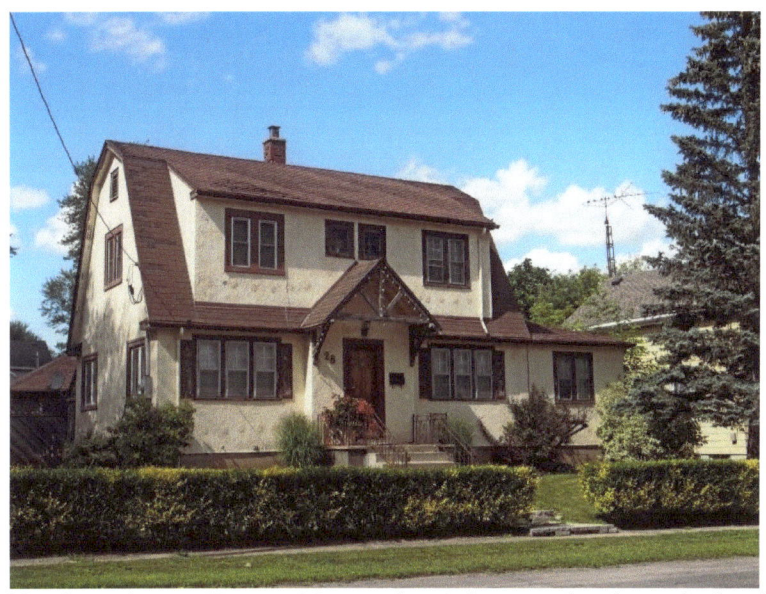

28 Elgin Street East – Neo-colonial – gambrel roof, shed dormer

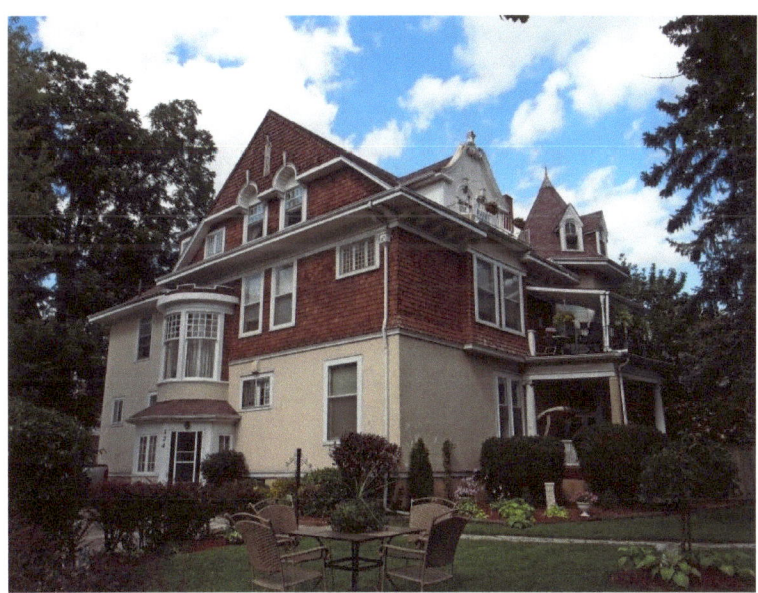

124 Elgin Street West – Queen Anne style, decorative dormer with walkout balcony, two-storey bay window

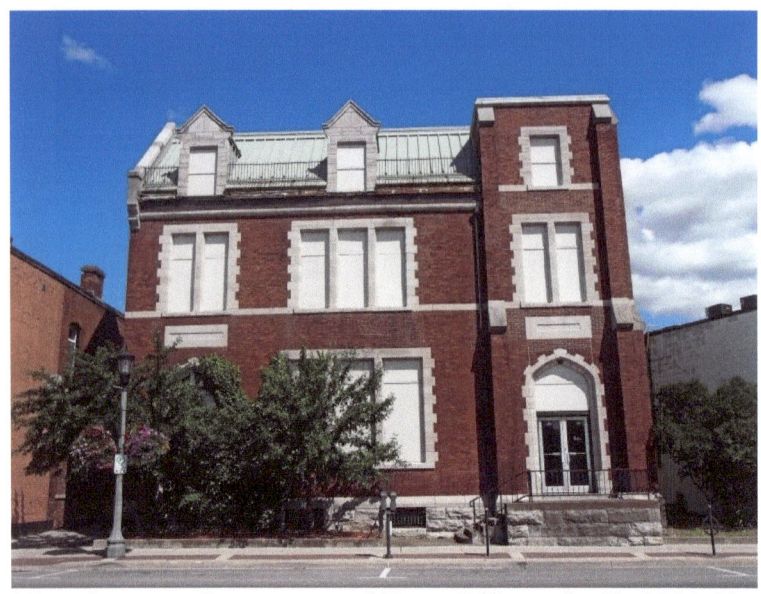

King Street – Customs and Post Office – built 1901-02 - quoining, buttresses, dormers – Welland Book 2

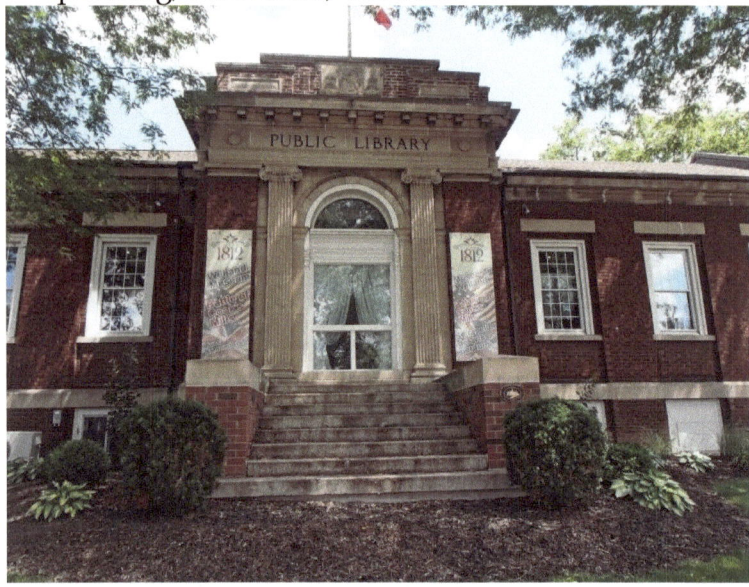

140 King Street – former Welland Public Library – 1923 – dark red Milton brick and Indiana limestone in the Beaux-Arts style

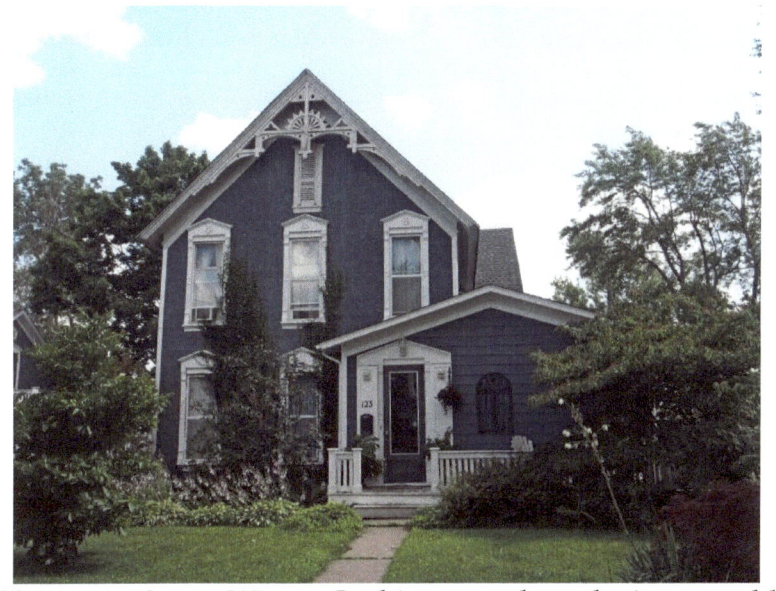

123 Merritt Street West – Gothic, verge board trim on gable

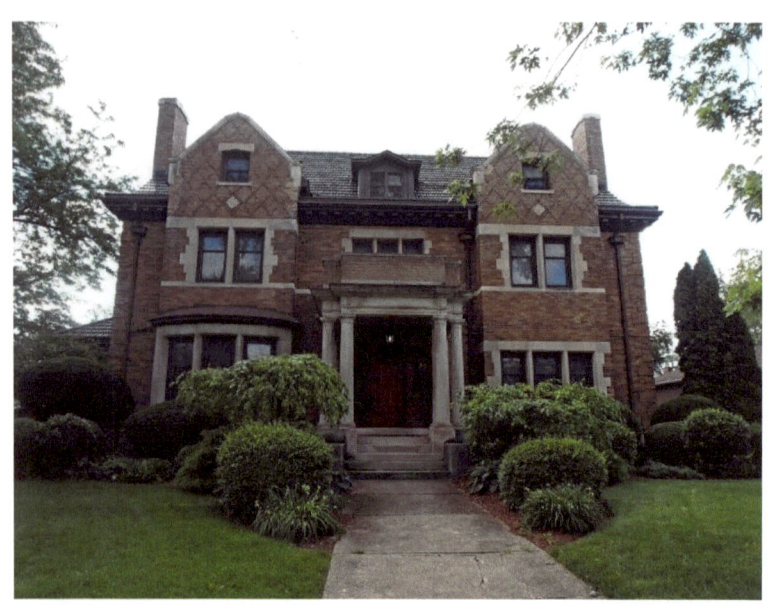

201 Niagara Street – Cooper Mansion – 1913-1914 - Renaissance Revival style, Jacobean gables (parapet), symmetrical façade with projecting wings, , dormers, stone trim, neoclassical doorway with elliptical fanlight and slender sidelights sheltered by a classical portico supported on six Doric columns

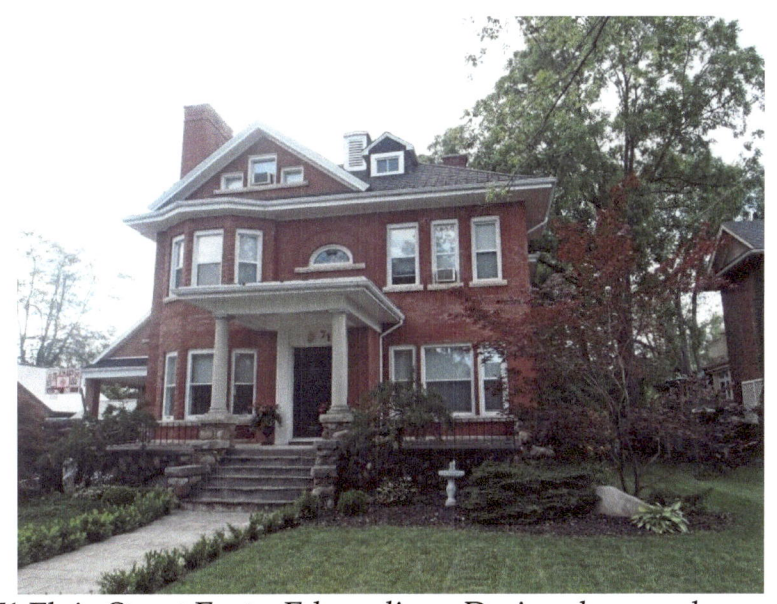

71 Elgin Street East – Edwardian - Doric columns, dormer, Palladian-type window in gable

Kingston, Ontario – My Top 23 Picks

In October 1783, at Carleton Island, Captain William Redford Carleton of the King's Royal Regiment of New York, met with the local Mississauga Indians led by the elderly Mynass. Crawford, acting for the British government, purchased from the Mississaugas for some clothing, ammunition and colored cloth, a large tract of land east of the Bay of Quinte. In September 1783, Deputy Surveyor-General John Collins was dispatched to Cataraqui by Governor Haldimand to lay out townships for Loyalist settlers. By the end of the year, the front concessions of four townships stretching from Cataraqui to the Bay of Quinte had been surveyed. A fifth township was laid out the following summer. The land was subsequently settled by United Empire Loyalists and Britain's allies who had been forced to leave their homes in the new United States.

Earl Street has a wide range of homes, some originally built for factory workers and others for the wealthy. They include a variety of frame, stone, stone and brick, and all-brick homes. They have different roof lines, porches, trim, chimneys, windows and transoms.

The Kingston Custom House was built 1856-59 for the government of the united Canadas. The symmetrical composition of the two-storey ashlar building, surmounted by a restrained cornice and parapet, draws on the British classical tradition. The orderly design is achieved through repeated use of semi-circular forms for doors and windows. The Custom House and the nearby Post Office are fine examples of the architectural quality of mid-nineteenth century administrative buildings.

The Kingston Penitentiary which opened on June 1, 1835 was Canada's oldest reformatory prison. Its layout – an imposing front gate leading to a cross-shaped cell block with workshops to the rear – was the model for other federal prisons for more than a century. It is Classical architecture in local stone.

Kingston Penitentiary represented a significant departure from the way society had dealt with its criminals. Previously, jails were used primarily as places to hold convicts awaiting execution, banishment, or public humiliation. The penitentiary imposed a severe regime designed to reform the inmate through reflection, hard work, and the fear of punishment. Inmates lived in small cells but worked together from dawn to dusk under a rigidly enforced code of silence. Kingston Penitentiary stands as a symbol of this country's commitment to maintaining law and order.

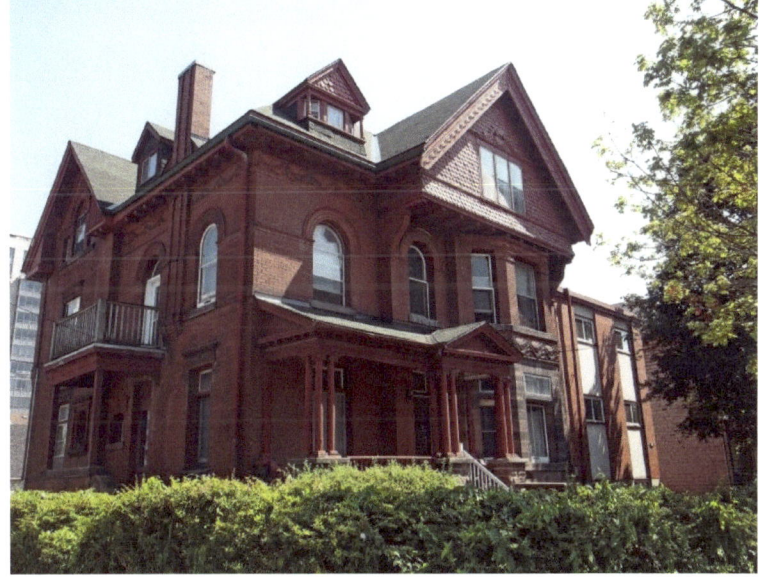

213 King Street East – Italianate – decorative brickwork below cornice and above first floor windows, dormers with fish scale pattern in the gables, pediment, columns with Ionic capitals supporting the verandah – Kingston Book 1

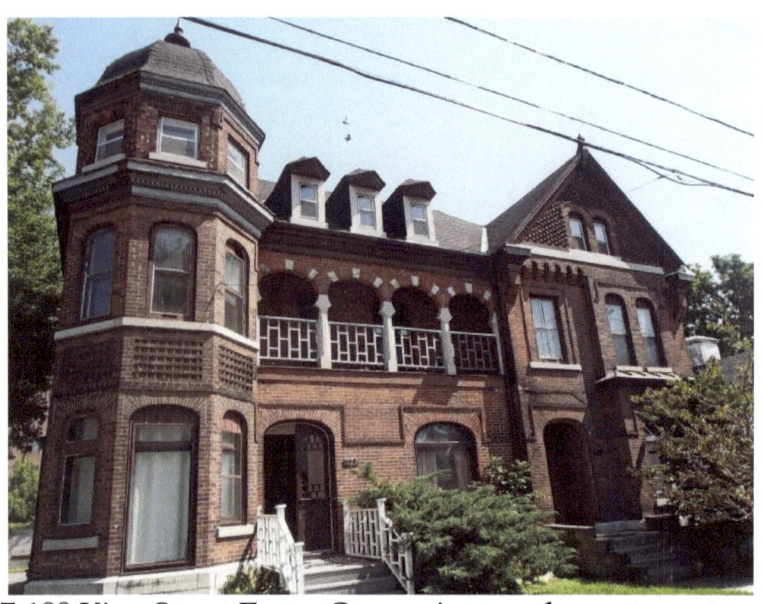

197-199 King Street East – Queen Anne – three-storey turret, dormers, second floor sleeping balcony, dichromatic voussoirs, decorative brickwork in large gable

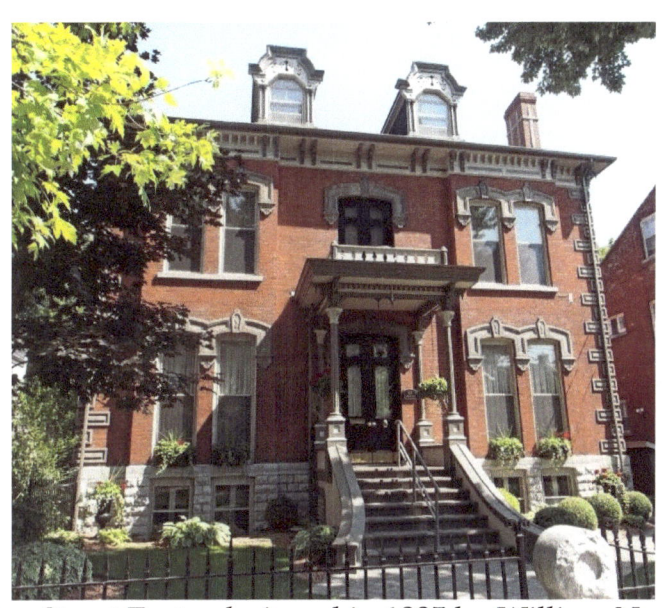

169 King Street East – designed in 1885 by William Newlands for banker Donald Fraser – three-bay, two-storey house is built on a high foundation; porch with paired columns on brick piers and a plain balustrade was added later; corner quoins with raised panels; channeled hood

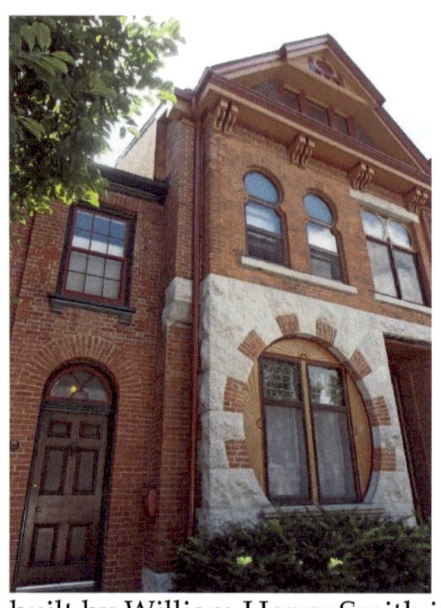

52 Earl Street – built by William Henry Smith in 1876 – Grove House – sunburst design on the façade; cornice brackets, oriel window, dormers

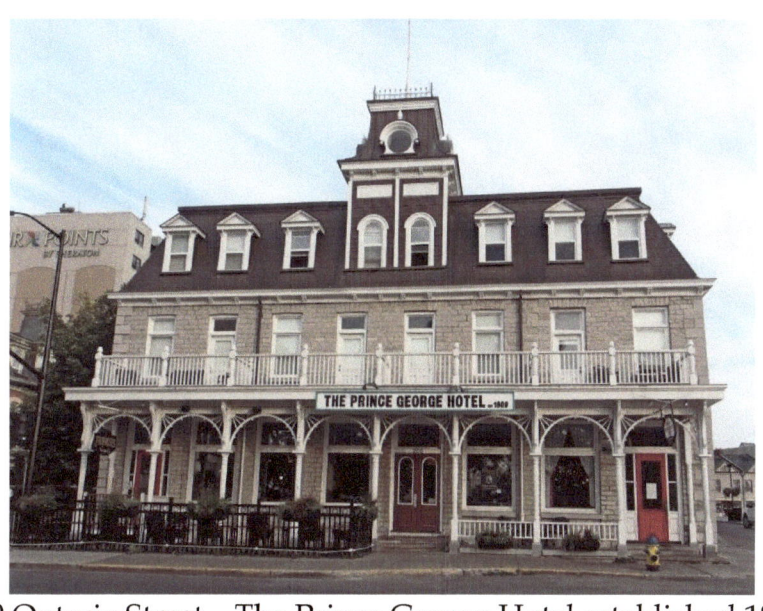

200 Ontario Street – The Prince George Hotel established 1809 – the façade is actually three separate buildings – the middle part is a stone house built about 1817; new stores were built on each side of the house in 1847 – later became a hotel – third floor with mansard roof added in 1892; iron cresting on the tower; copper roof; decorative woodwork on verandah – Kingston Book 2

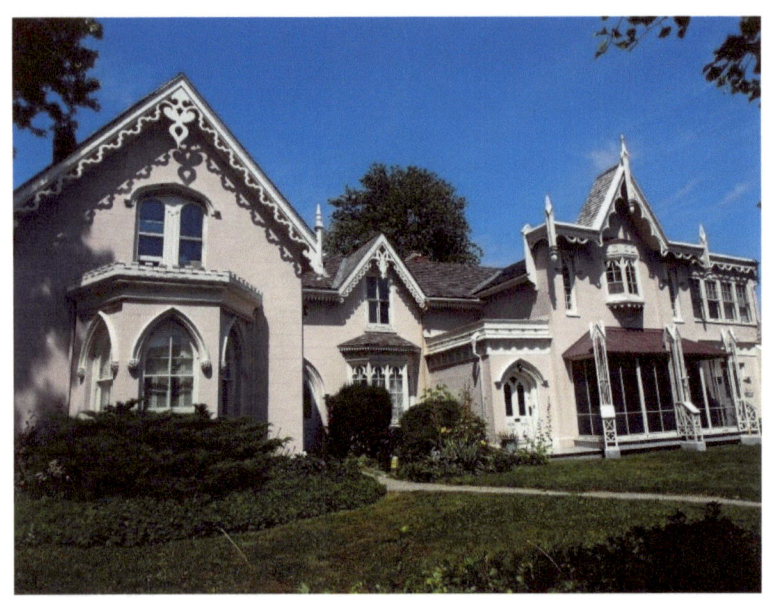

251 Brock Street - Elizabeth Cottage - Gothic Revival style – built 1840s – steeply pointed gables, projecting bays, oriel windows – accentuate play of light and shadow on smooth stucco walls; applied Gothic decorative details such as verge board trim, crockets, finials and drip moldings heighten the picturesque effect

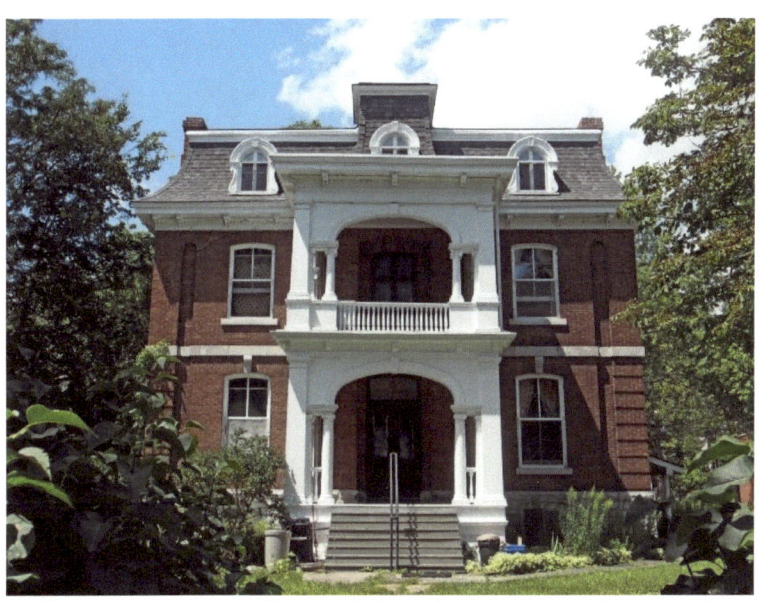

12 Wellington Street – Second Empire, mansard roof, dormers with window hoods, two-storey central verandahs – Doric columns on first storey with semi-circular arch with keystone; Ionic columns on second storey with identical arch

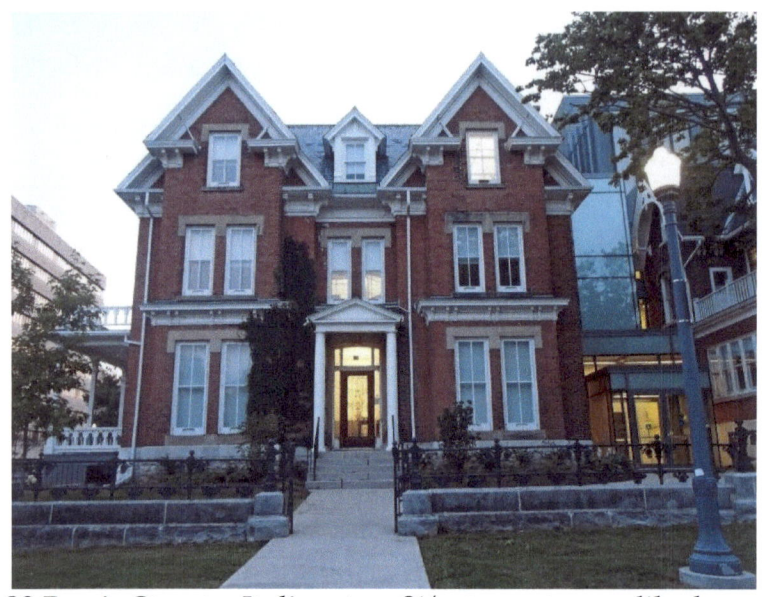

80 Barrie Street – Italianate – 2½-storey tower-like bays, cornice return on gables, dormer between gables, cornice brackets, pediment above door, sidelights and transom – Kingston Book 3

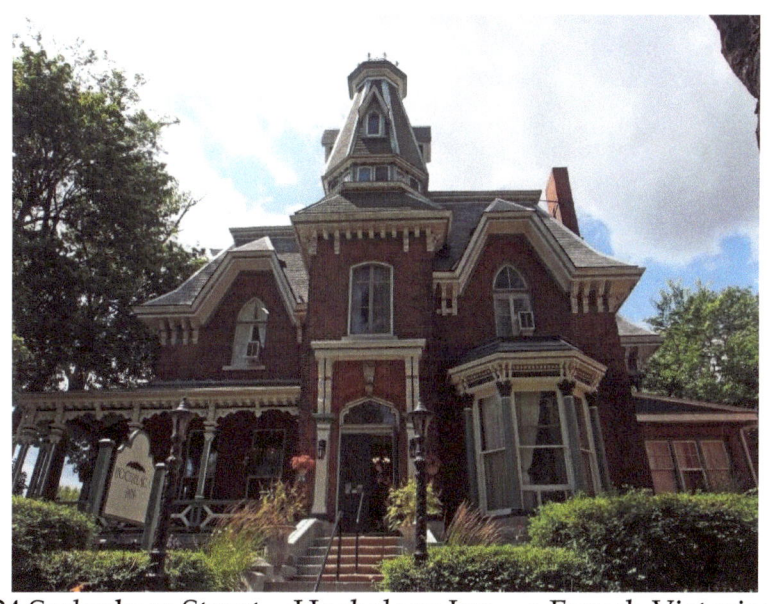

24 Sydenham Street – Hochelaga Inn – a French Victorian mansion built in 1879 by John McIntyre and his wife Harriet, who was a relative of Sir John A. Macdonald – transformed into an inn in 1985 – three-storey tower, cornice brackets, bay window

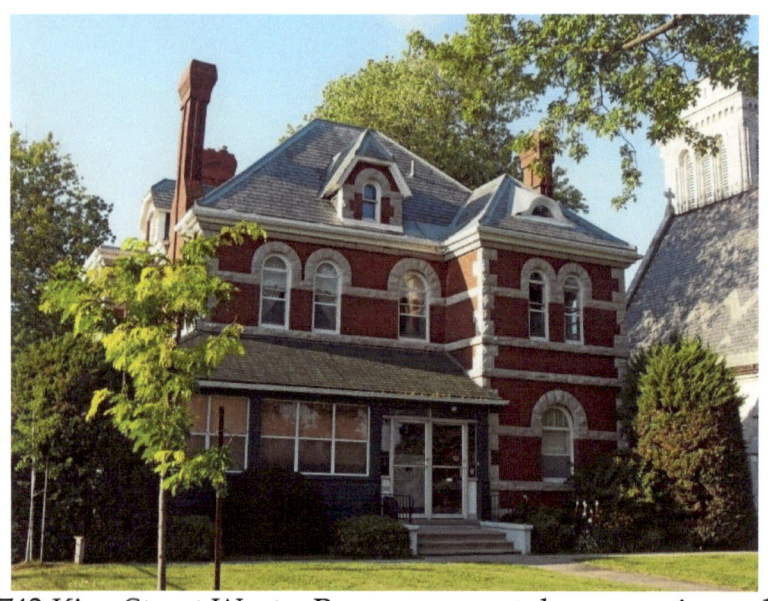

743 King Street West – Romanesque style, voussoirs and banding, gabled dormer, eyebrow dormer, tall chimneys, corner quoins – Kingston Book 4

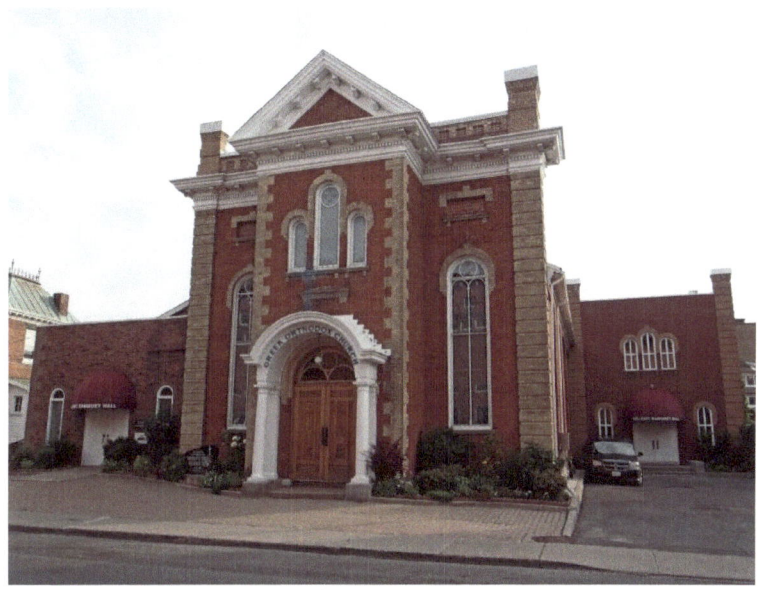

121 Johnson Street – Greek Orthodox Church – Romanesque style - two-storey frontispiece topped with pediment, corner quoins, dentil molding

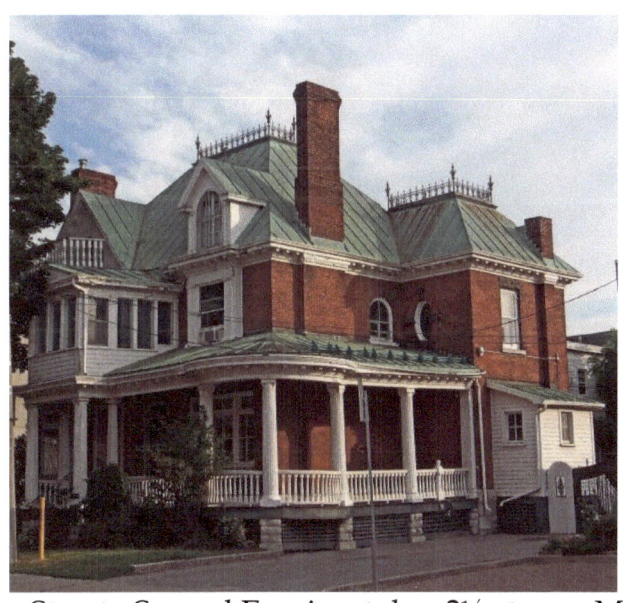

Johnson Street - Second Empire style – 2½ storey, Mansard roof, dormers, iron cresting on roof, wraparound verandah

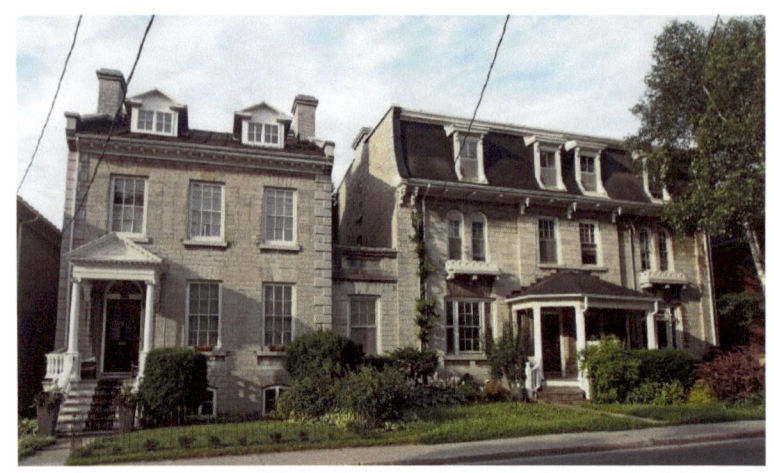

222 Johnson Street; 226 Johnson Street – Mansard-like roof with dormers, semi-circular and rectangular windows

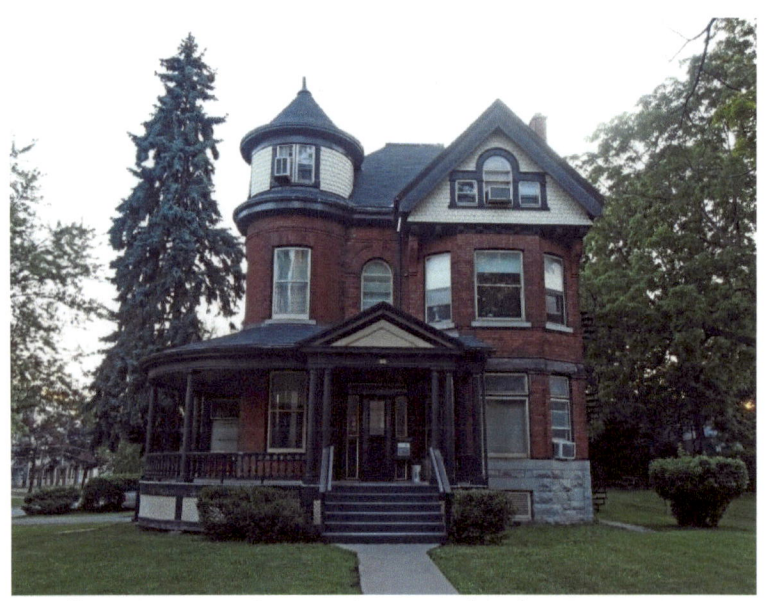

96 Albert Street – Queen Anne style, three-storey turret, Palladian window above two-storey bay window, pediment, voussoirs with keystone – Kingston Book 5

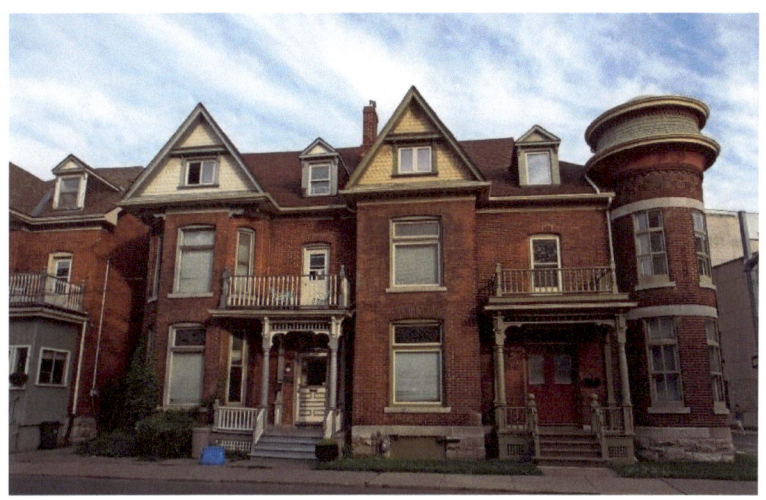

208-210 Bagot Street – Edwardian, two-storey tower-like bay, dormers

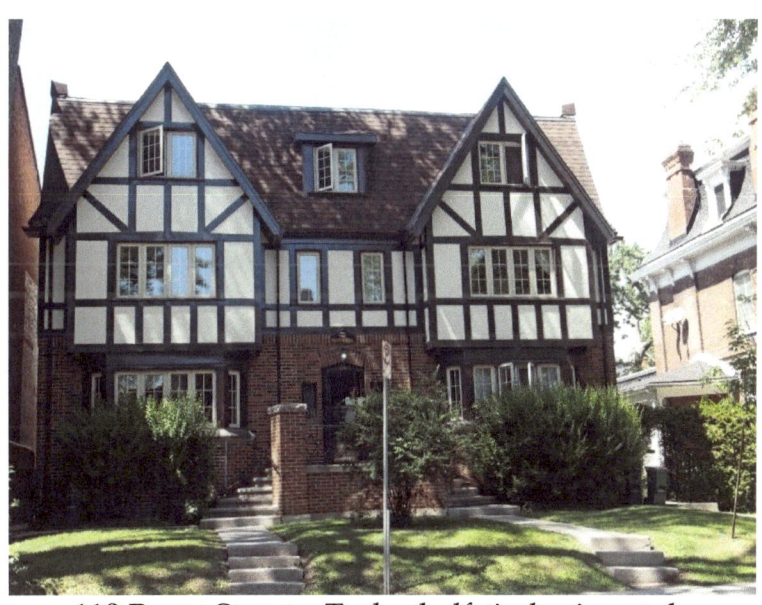

110 Bagot Street – Tudor half-timbering style

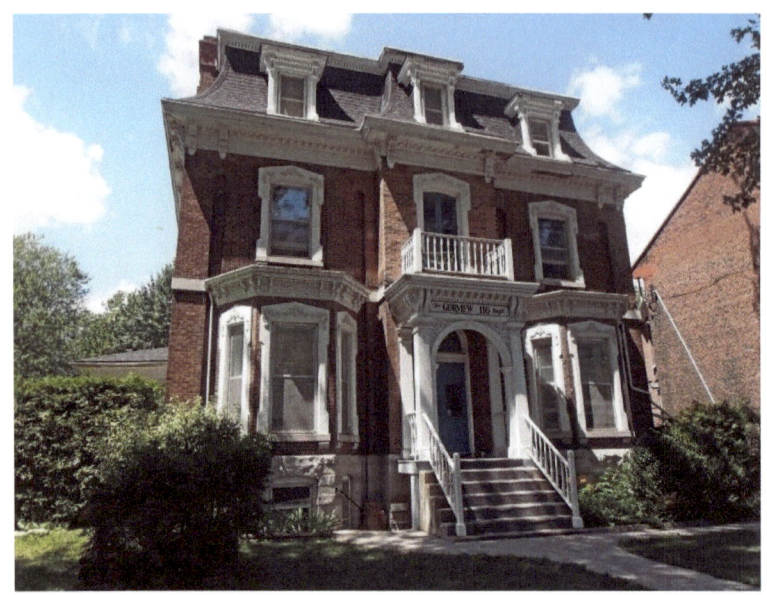

116 Bagot Street – Second Empire, Mansard roof with dormers and window hoods, second floor balcony, bay windows, cornice brackets, dentil molding, pillared entrance

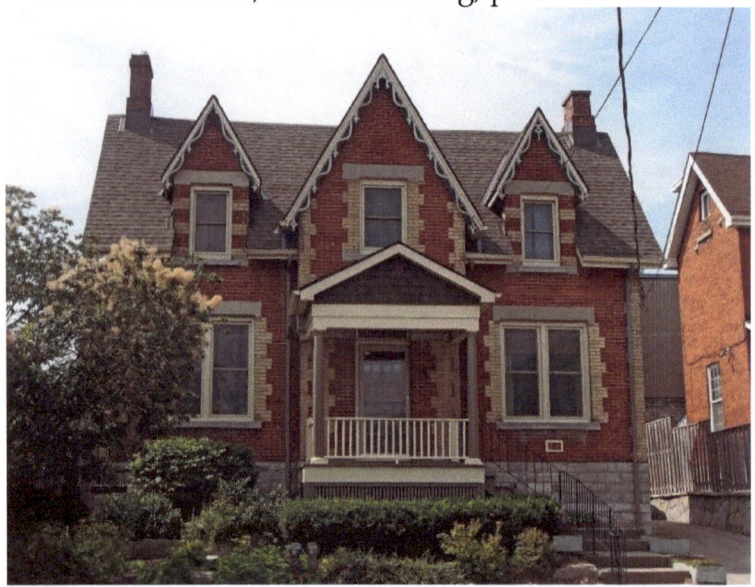

164 Queen Street – Gothic Revival – verge board trim on gables, corner quoins, and dichromatic brickwork

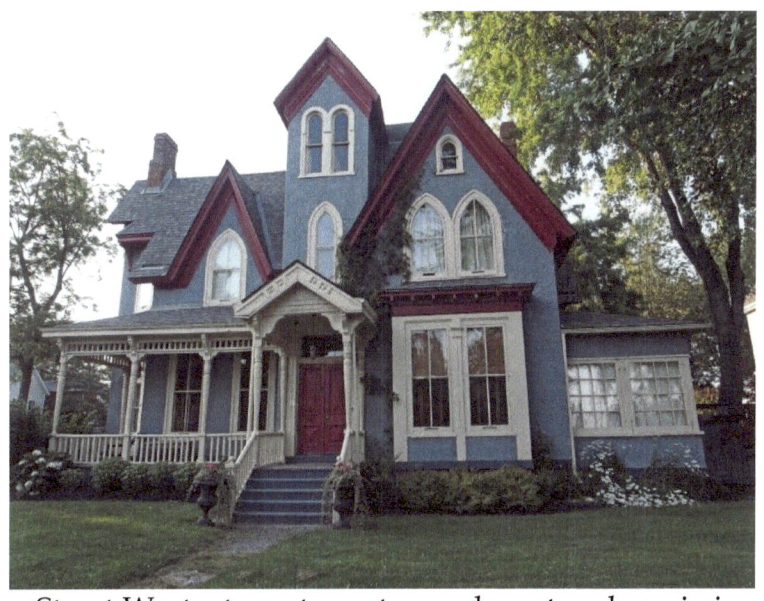

King Street West – two-storey tower, lancet and semi-circular windows, transom window above door – Kingston Book 6

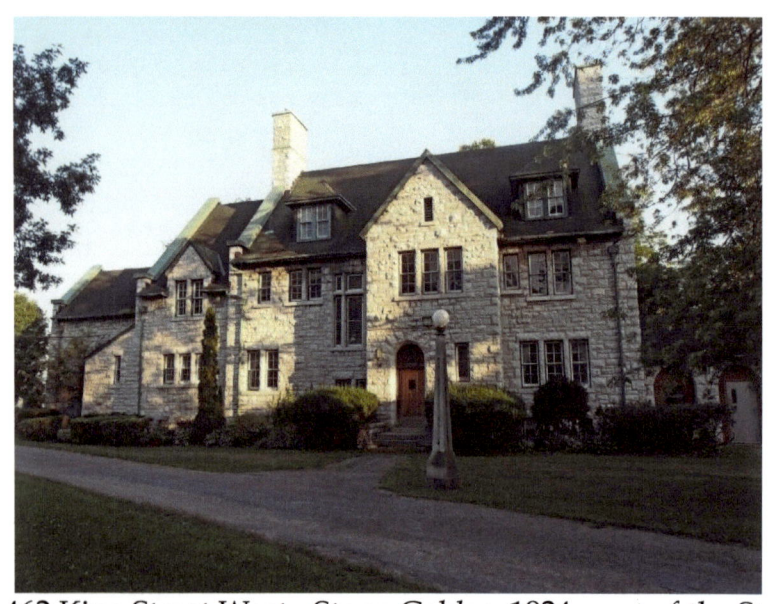

462 King Street West - Stone Gables, 1924, part of the St. Helen's Complex, is located on landscaped grounds bordering Lake Ontario. The grand, Tudor Revival, stone building features a steeply pitched gable roof, a projecting gabled frontispiece, prominent gable chimneys, and hipped dormer windows.

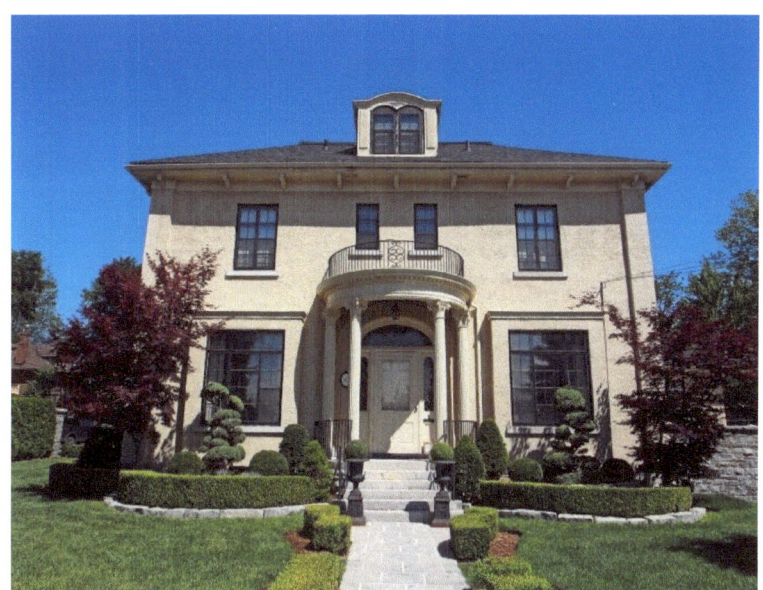

163 Union Street – two storeys, hipped roof with dormer, four Corinthian pillars supporting a semi-circular roof with balcony above, dentil molding, sidelights and transom windows around door

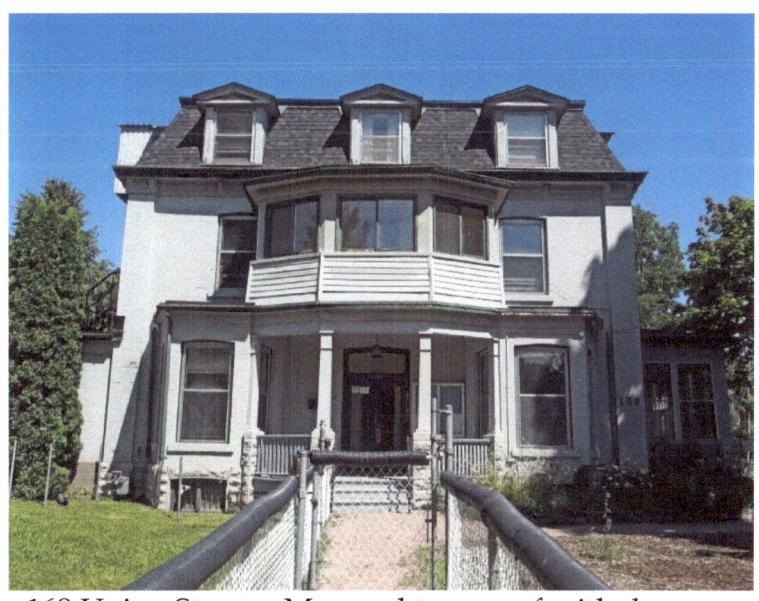

169 Union Street – Mansard-type roof with dormers

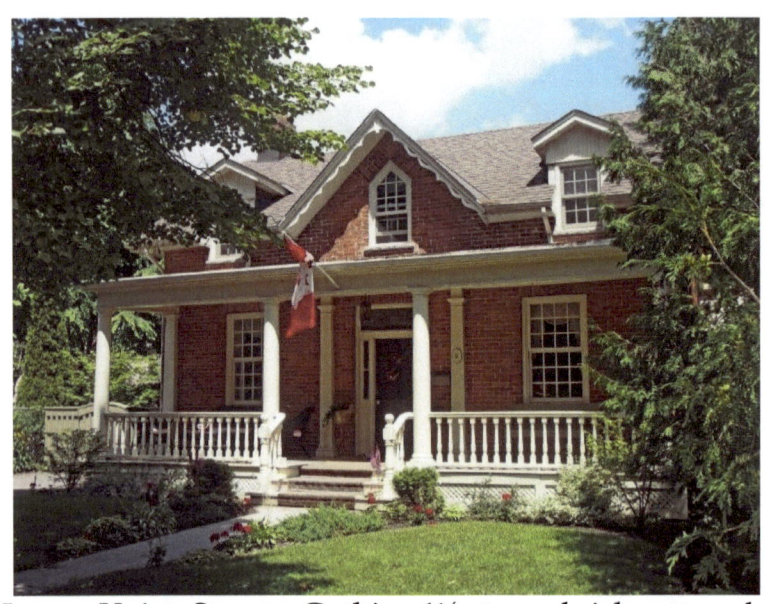

81 Lower Union Street – Gothic - 1½ storey brick cottage built in 1875 – narrow sidelight windows, porch with Doric pillars – carved wooden bargeboard on gable, dormers

Ottawa, Ontario – My Top 11 Picks

After the union of the two Canadas in 1841, Kingston, Montreal, Toronto and Quebec were in succession the seat of government. During the 1850s these cities contended for designation as the permanent capital of Canada. During Queen Victoria's long reign, the nation of Canada was created, grew and flourished. Queen Victoria ascended the throne in 1837, the same year that violent rebellions broke out in Upper and Lower Canada with demands for a more democratic and responsible form of government. These rebellions prompted many reforms, including the unification of Upper and Lower Canada into the Province of Canada. In 1857, Queen Victoria chose Ottawa as Canada's capital, a political compromise as well as a more secure distance from the American border. In 1867, Queen Victoria signed the *British North America Act* to create the Dominion of Canada, a self-governing nation within the British Empire, established through peaceful accord and negotiation. The Fathers of Confederation reaffirmed the choice and Ottawa as the capital for the new Dominion.

Parliament Hill sits at the heart of Canada's Capital, overlooking a river that reflects many histories. From the beginning, Parliament Hill was designed as a workplace for parliamentarians, and also as a place where everyone could come to meet, talk or just relax in a beautiful outdoor setting. Today there is a scenic promenade which follows the shoreline of the Ottawa River.

The Centre, East and West blocks of the Parliament Buildings were built between 1859 and 1866 (excluding the Tower and Library). The Parliament Buildings have vaulted ceilings, marble floors and dramatic lighting which create an air of dignity. The stone walls have a lot of decoration.

Sir John A. Macdonald (1815-1891) was one of the driving forces behind Confederation in Canada, with Nova Scotia, New Brunswick, Ontario and Quebec joining together to form a new country. Macdonald served as the country's first prime minister. Manitoba, British Columbia and Prince Edward Island entered Confederation under his government, while the last spike of the Canadian Pacific Railway's transcontinental line was hammered into the ground.

The Rideau Canal, a great military engineering achievement of the nineteenth century, was completed in 1832 and opened central Canada to settlement and trade. The canal was planned after the War of 1812 to provide a safe way to transport troops and equipment between Montreal and Kingston. The entrance locks mark the beginning of a 202-kilometer route linking the Ottawa River and Lake Ontario through a system of lakes and rivers connected and made navigable by the channels, locks and dams that the workers constructed.

In the 1890s, when Prime Minister Sir Wilfrid Laurier spoke of making Ottawa a "Washington of the North", he wanted a new architectural style for the Capital that was distinct from American and older British models, in pursuit of grandeur.

In 1982, the Queen and the Right Honorable Pierre Trudeau, Prime Minister, signed the *Constitution Act, 1982* to make Canada an independent nation.

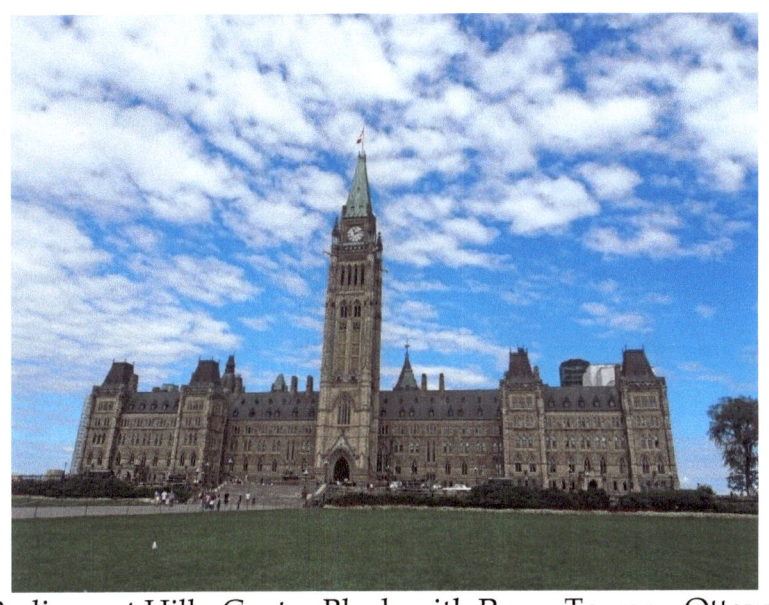

Parliament Hill - Centre Block with Peace Tower – Ottawa
Book 1

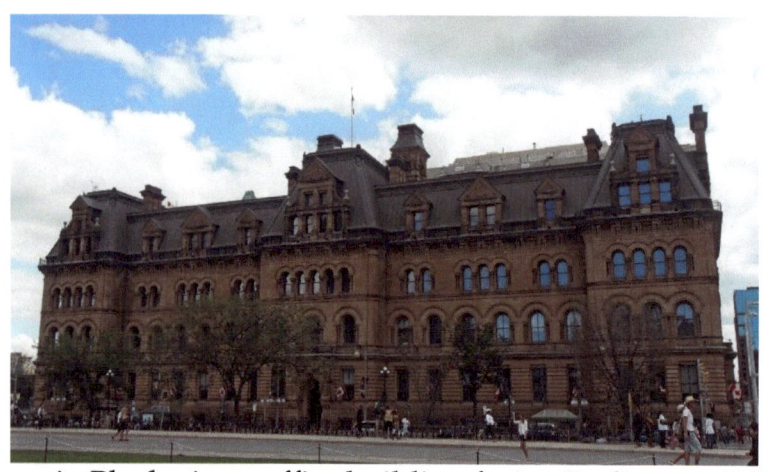

Langevin Block - is an office building facing Parliament Hill. As the home of the Privy Council Office and Office of the Prime Minister, it is the working headquarters of the executive branch of the Canadian government. The building is named after a Father of Confederation and cabinet minister Hector Langevin. Built of sandstone from a New Brunswick quarry between 1884 and 1889 - Second Empire style - Mansard roof, dormers, grotesque sculptures (fantastic or mythical figures used for decorative purposes)

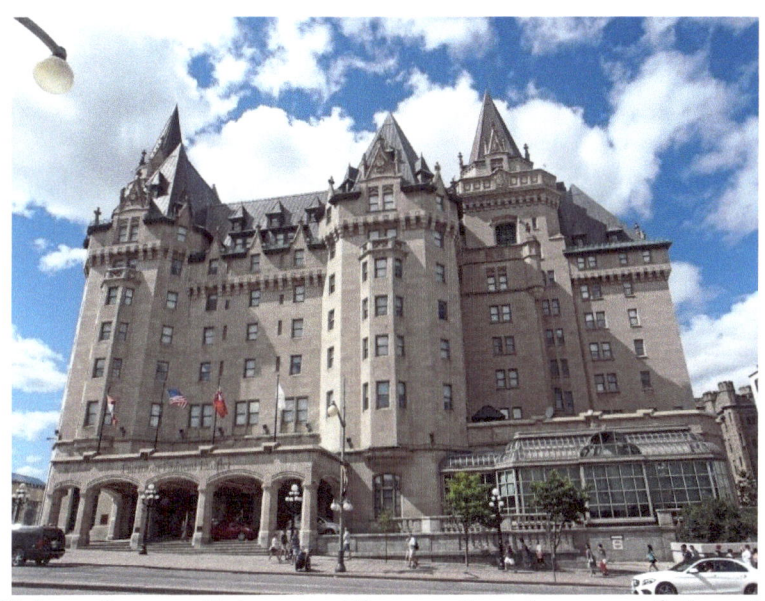

1 Rideau Street - Fairmont Chateau Laurier, one of Canada's landmark railway hotels, built in the Canadian Chateau style

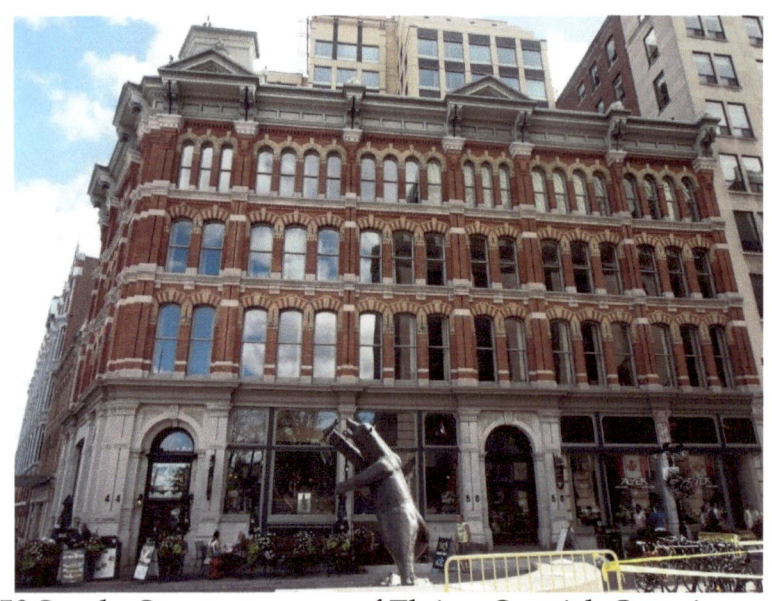

44-50 Sparks Street at corner of Elgin – Scottish Ontario Chambers – Italianate design - four-storey brick building with a high ground floor, balanced façade, decorative multi-colored masonry, radiated voussoirs of multicolored brick, fenestration (the arrangement, design and proportioning of windows and doors), roof line with heavy bracketing and decorated cornice – Ottawa Book 2

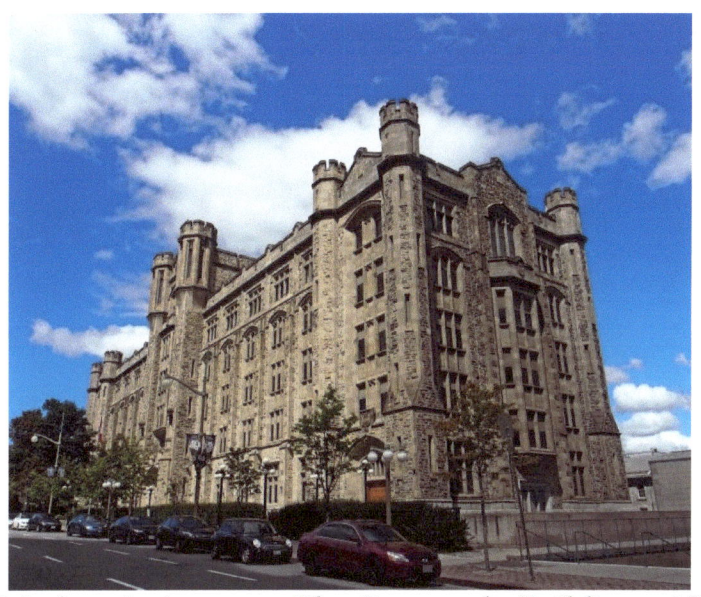

555 Mackenzie Avenue – The Connaught Building – 1913 – Tudor Gothic - named after the Duke of Connaught, third son of Queen Victoria, who served as 10th Governor General of Canada from 1911–16 – faced in rusticated sandstone, embellished with turrets, a crenellated roofline, buttresses, corbelling, niches, carved embellishments, an ogee arched entrance and rows of flat-headed windows accented by dressed quoins

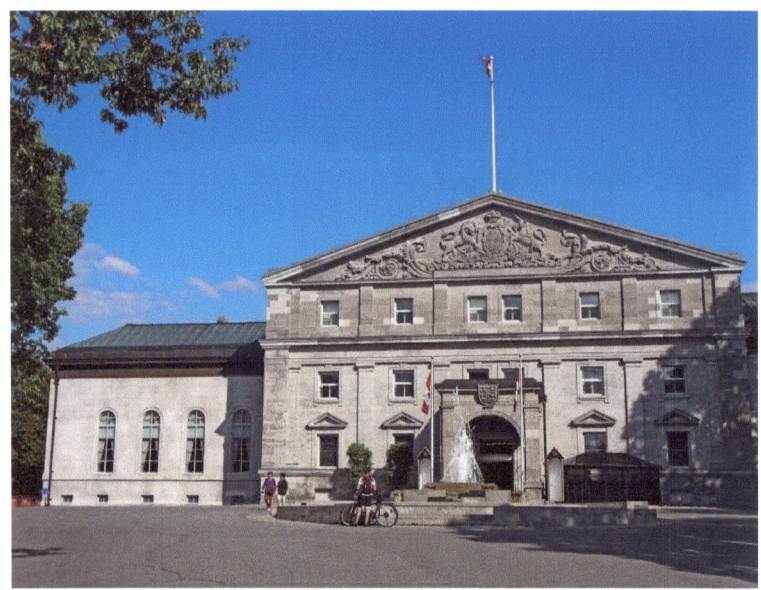

Rideau Hall - Thomas MacKay, a wealthy Scottish stonemason and entrepreneur, helped build the Rideau Canal. Following the completion of the canal, McKay built mills at Rideau Falls, making him the founder of New Edinburgh, the original settlement of Ottawa. With his newly acquired wealth, McKay purchased the 100 acre site overlooking both the Ottawa and Rideau Rivers and built a stone villa in 1838 where he and his family lived until 1855. The building, an eleven-room mansion, was known as MacKay Castle. Following Confederation, Rideau Hall was purchased by the Canadian government as a permanent vice regal residence and home for the nation's first governor general, Lord Monck. Subsequent governor generals expanded and improved the original building to carry out their increasing official duties. Lord Dufferin added the wings on either side of the main entrance in the 1870s. – Ottawa Book 3

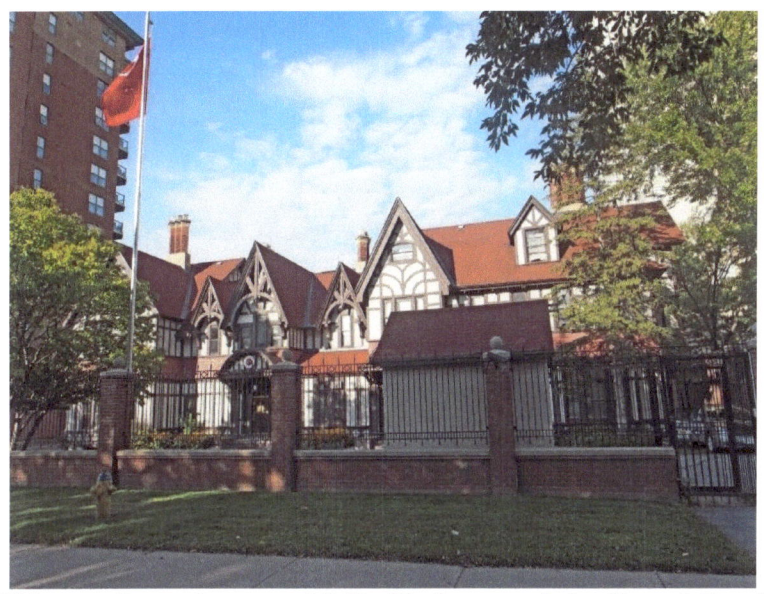

197 Wurtemburg Street – 1869 - Embassy of the Republic of Turkey - Tudor style – The central portion of the building was a picturesque Gothic Revival structure constructed for W.F. Whitcher, Commissioner of Fisheries. The two wings and the Tudoresque half-timbering were added when the structure served as a Children's Hospital from 1888-1904.

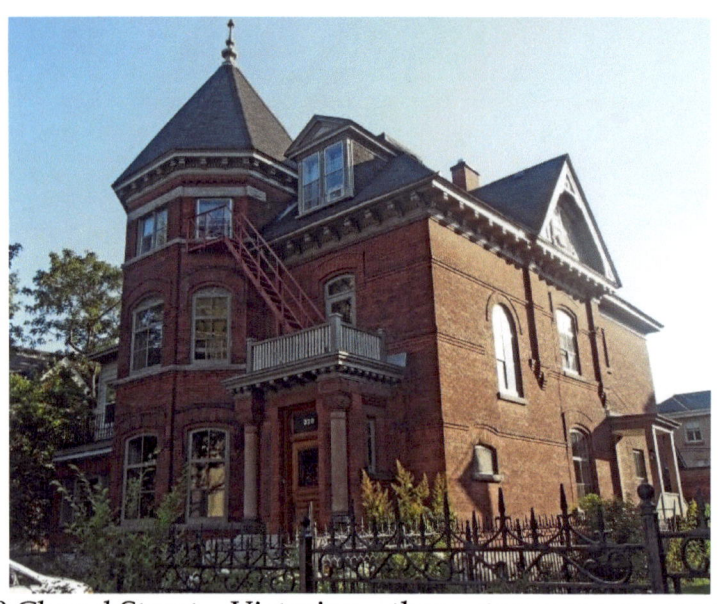

320 Chapel Street – Victorian – three-storey tower, cornice brackets, gable, voussoirs, banding, dormer, composite columns around door – Ottawa Book 4

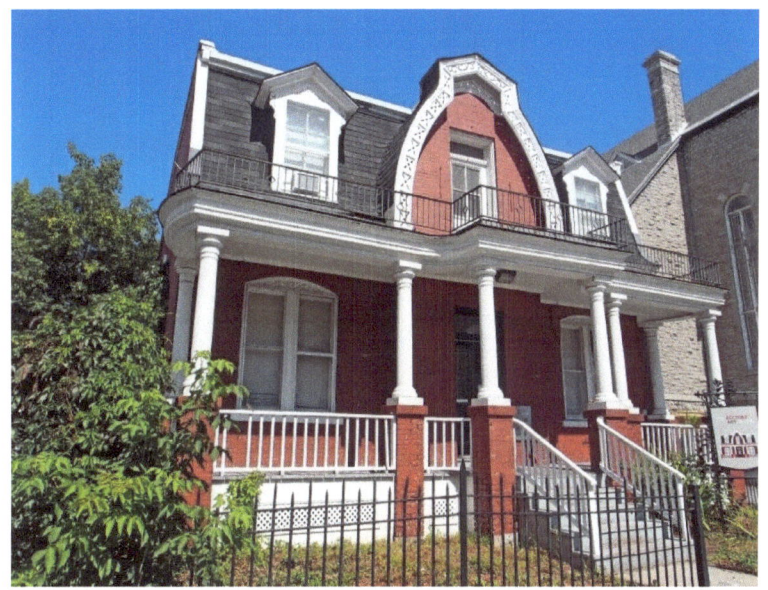

179 Murray Street – a small house of **9 artist studios -** aiding the city of Ottawa in developing an artistic and cultural identity – window hoods, Jacobean-type gable, Doric pillars

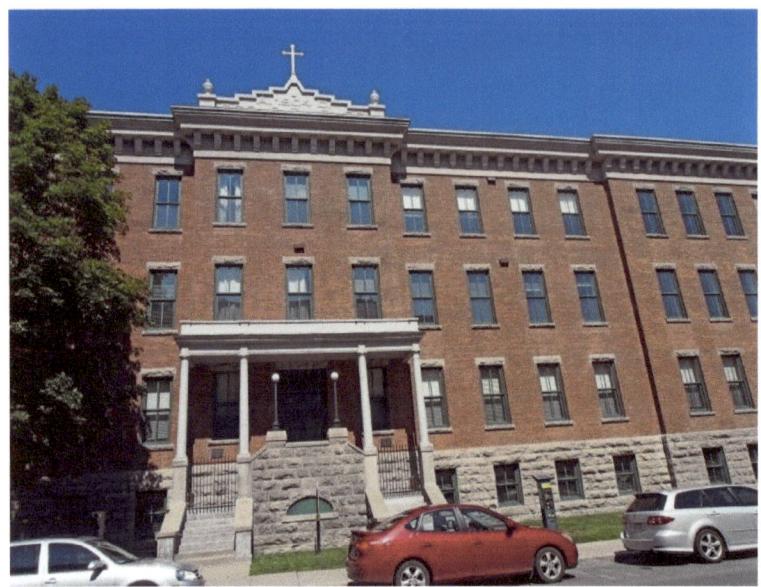

159 Murray Street - Ecole Guigues – The current building opened its doors in 1904 and was one of Ottawa's largest schools. Two sisters, Diane Desloges and Beatrice Desloges, natives of Ottawa and both teachers at the Guigues elementary school, refused to implement the provisions of Regulation 17, thus defying the ministerial order [issued by the Ontario Ministry of Education] that limited teaching in French to the first two years of elementary school. On January 5, 1916, the Ottawa Separate School Board, with nineteen mothers and the Desloges sisters, stormed the entrance of this school to demand that Franco-Ontarian pupils be educated in their mother tongue. It was not until 1927 that bilingual schools in the province were officially recognized. Thousands of students passed through its halls until it closed in 1979.

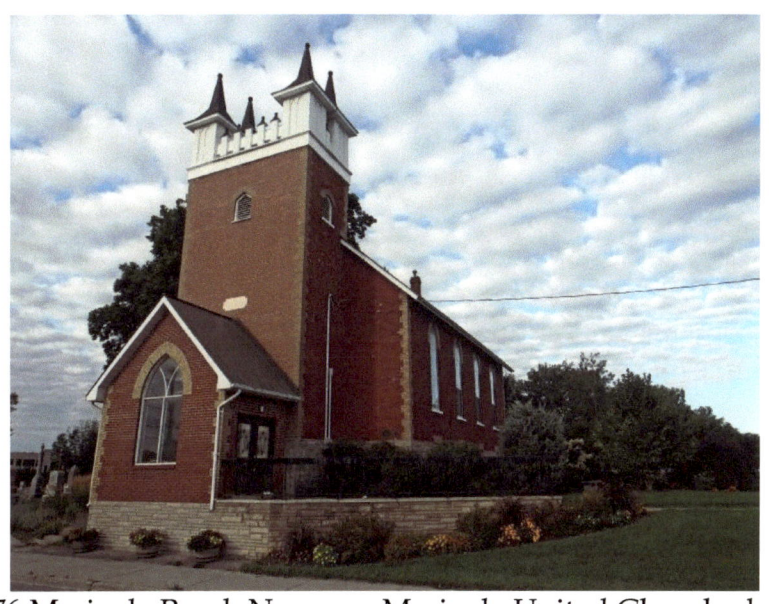

1876 Merivale Road, Nepean - Merivale United Church - built 1875-1876 – Gothic Revival – finials on tower with balustrade; corner quoins

Midland, Ontario – My Top 15 Picks

Midland is located on the southern end of Georgian Bay's 30,000 Islands about ninety miles north of Toronto.

Huronia was named for the Huron Nation and consists of the areas around southeastern Georgian Bay which include Midland and Penetanguishene. The area was visited by French Jesuits traveling with the Voyageurs to the Wye River in 1639. They were welcomed by the Huron tribe who traded furs and skins for metal goods and clothing from France. They built a settlement named Fort Ste. Marie which thrived for ten years until it was burned to the ground in 1649 by the Jesuits themselves after repeated attacks from Iroquois who were in league with the English who wanted the French share of the fur trade in North America. Some of the priests were martyred. The Sainte-Marie among the Hurons site was discovered in 1947, excavated and rebuilt to its original form by archeologists from the University of Western Ontario.

The Jesuits attempted a second site on St. Joseph's Island, currently Christian Island, and named it Sainte Marie II. They carried many of their goods by raft to this second site. After a winter of terrible hardship and starvation, the Jesuits decided to abandon their mission and returned to Quebec in 1650. Christian Island was later declared a native reservation by the Canadian government.

In 1871 a group of the principal shareholders of the Midland Railway, headed by Adolph Hugel, chose this location as the northern terminus of their line which they ran from Port Hope to Beaverton. The town site was surveyed in 1872-73. The railway line was completed in 1879 and soon attracted settlers to the area. The new community, Midland, achieved its early growth through shipping and the lumber and grain trade.

In and around the center of Midland there are a number of murals most of which were painted by now deceased artist Fred Lenz.

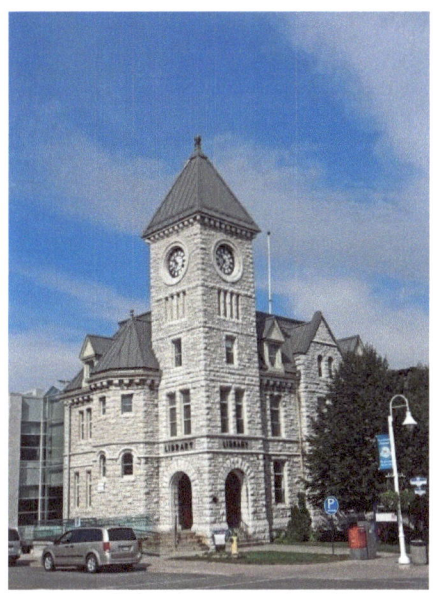

320 King Street - The impressive Romanesque style limestone structure which now houses the library was built in 1913 as Midland's first post office, with customs and excise offices on the second floor. - mansard roof, high central gable, imposing corner porch, and tower; 2½ storey building composed of even course cut stone, with a belt course that goes around the entire building; metal roof has a decorative stone fascia; some semi-elliptical windows, and a corner entrance. In 1963 the post office, needing more space, moved to its new home on Dominion Avenue and the beautiful limestone building sat empty for three years. In 1967, the library moved to the old post office. Setting your watch by the clock tower would be inadvisable as the four faces do not always agree. – Midland Book 1

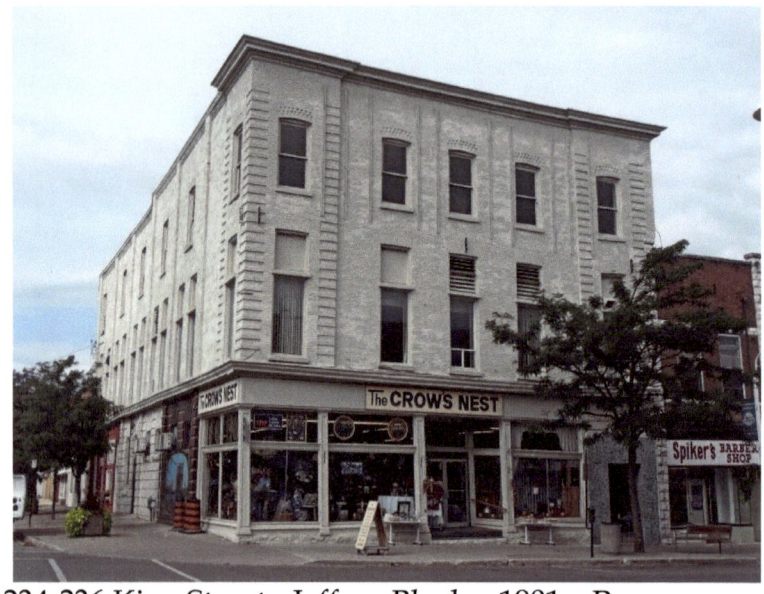

234-236 King Street - Jeffery Block – 1901 – Romanesque Revival style - large number and regular rhythm of windows; extend brick corner quoins and varied brick courses on the window lintels - The Crow's Nest Pub and Restaurant is now where the hardware store was; second floor YMCA; top floor Odd Fellows lodge meeting rooms

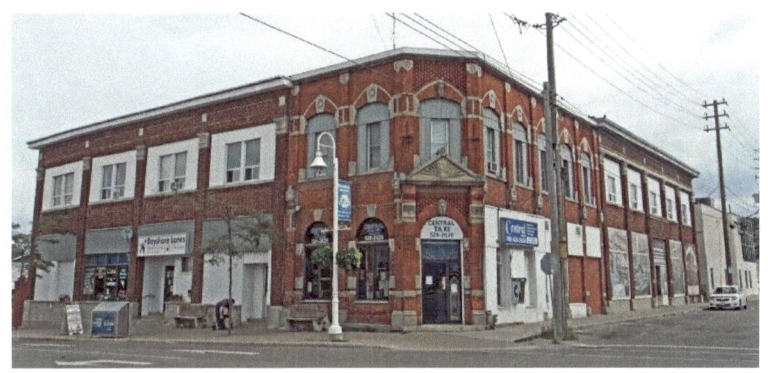

203-207 King Street - two storey, flat roofed commercial building - Burton Block, built by the Burton Brothers of Barrie - exterior of the building is made up of board and batten, stretcher brick, poured concrete, and sheet metal siding; frontispiece and decorated panels; brick keystones above windows; blind transom above door. The original stone carvings of Greek gods are still intact above the Taxi Stand door.

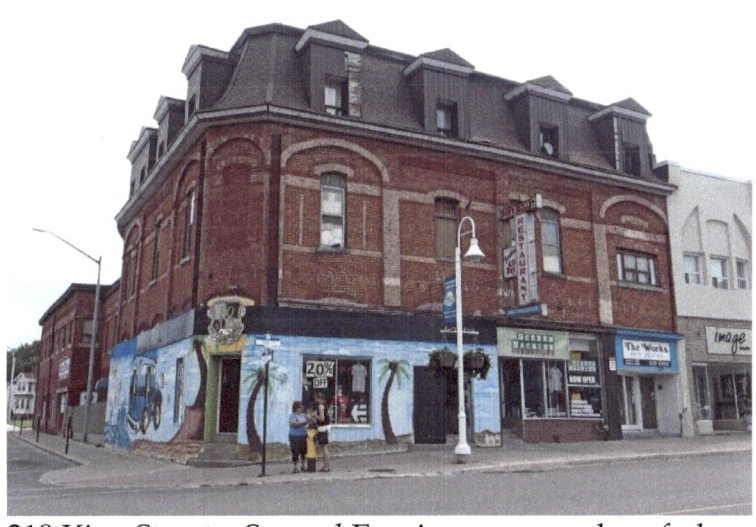

213-219 King Street – Second Empire – mansard roof, dormers, dichromatic brickwork

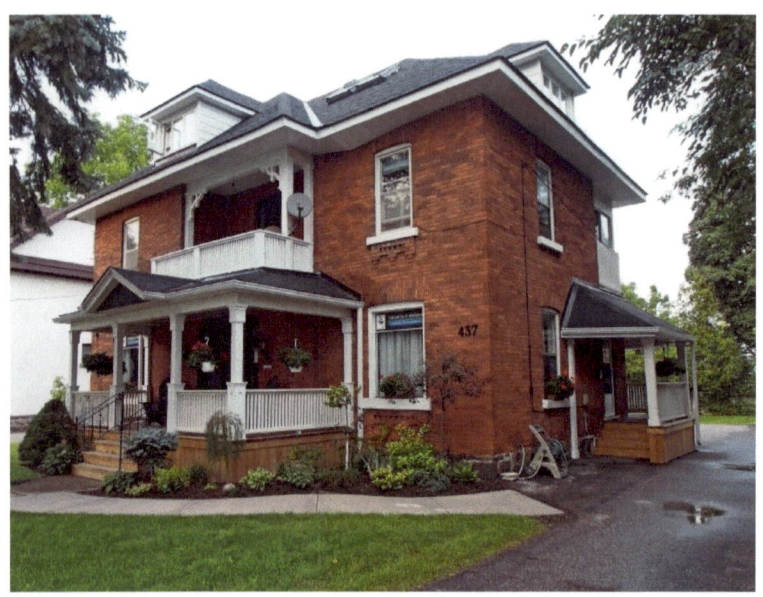

437 King Street - exterior is stretcher brick with a cut stone foundation; medium hipped roof and two second storey balconies; brick voussoirs; decorative brick below some windows; sidelights; open verandah with open railings and wood piers

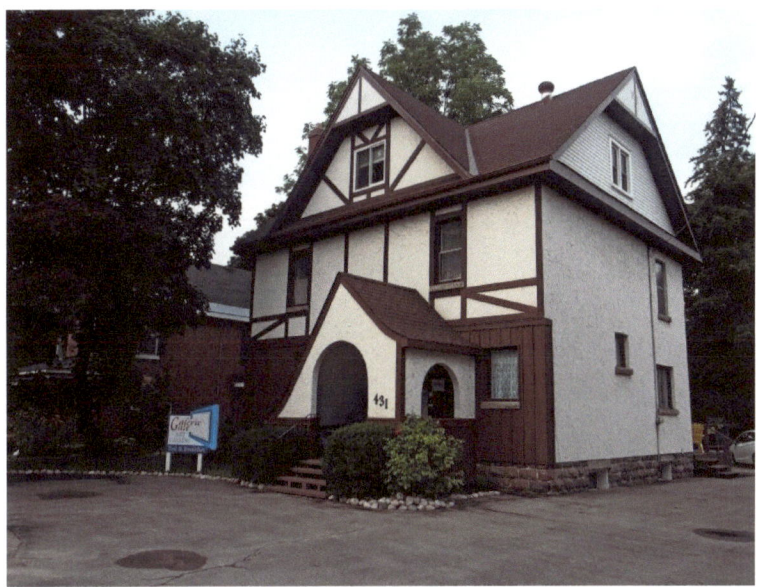

431 King Street - full basement; low gable roof with a double gable on the façade with a molded fascia; exterior is finished with log; main entrance has an ogee shaped opening with a plain pediment roof above and wood piers on sides

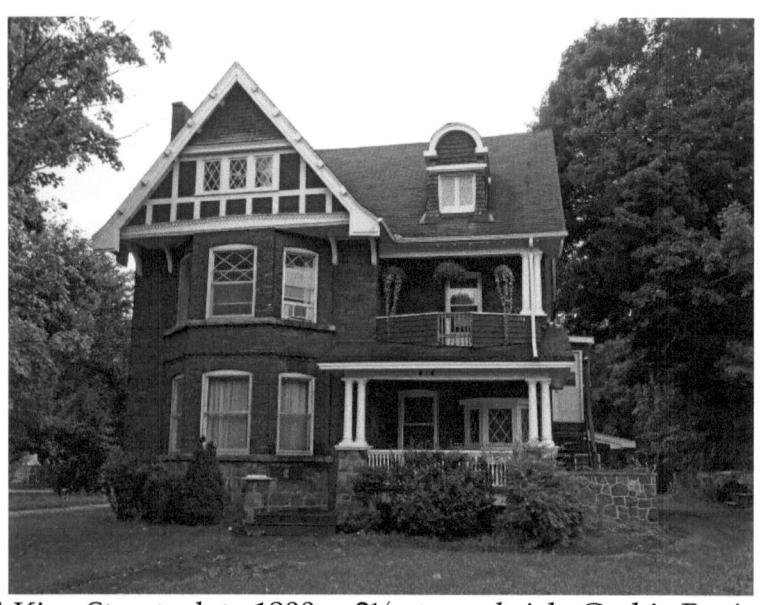

414 King Street – late 1800s - 2½ storey brick, Gothic Revival - dichromatic brick patterns, roof gables and dormer with rounded roof, various window shapes and sizes, mixed design verge boards and verandas

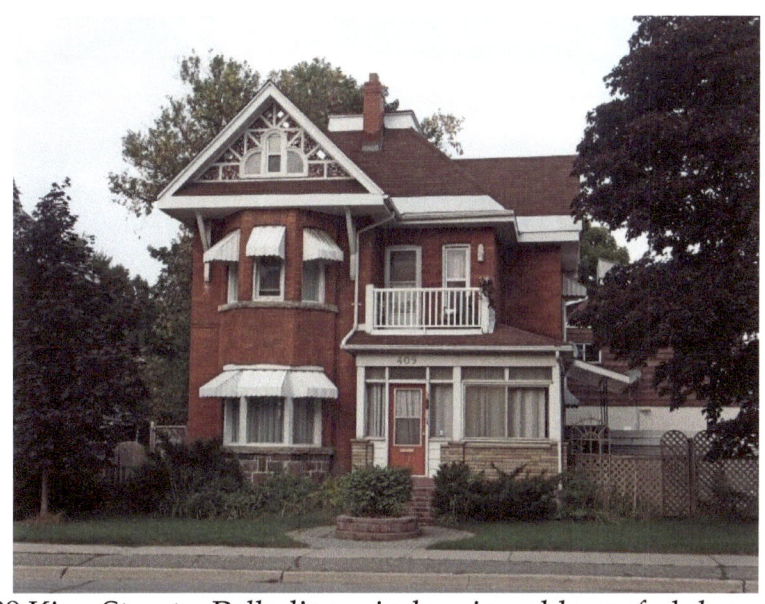

409 King Street – Palladian window in gable roofed dormer; two-storey bay window; second floor balcony above closed in porch; varied roofline

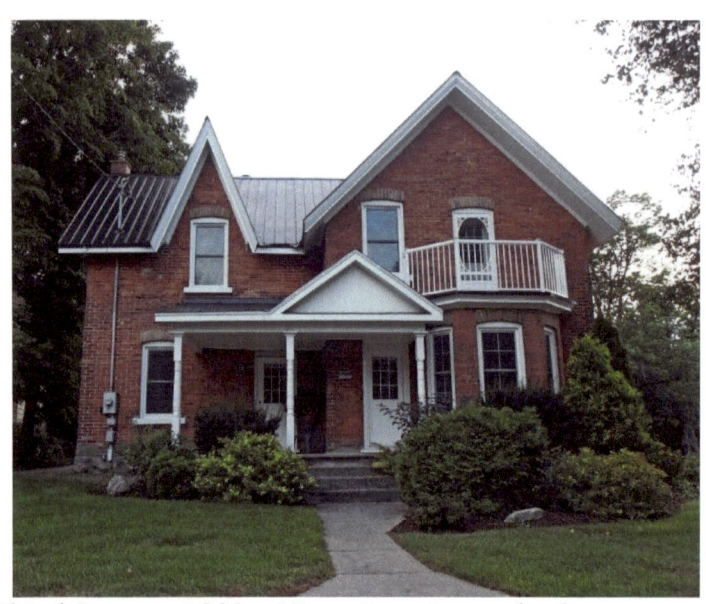

318 Third Street – 1900 – Victorian - irregular layout; medium gabled roof; double gable on façade; fascia and soffit are molded metal; exterior is stretcher brick and vertical plank board; two balconies; brick voussoirs; 4-over-4 window panes; blind transom; open porch with wood posts and pediment – Midland Book 2

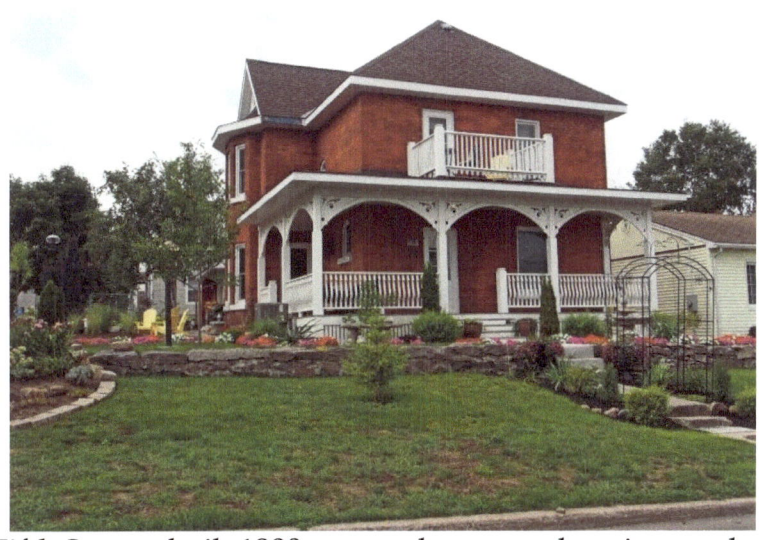

70 Fifth Street - built 1900, square layout and a wing on the left side; exterior is stretcher brick; upper storey balcony; medium hipped roof has an offset gable end on the façade and a molded frieze; semi-elliptical window on the left; open wooden veranda with decorative railings and support posts

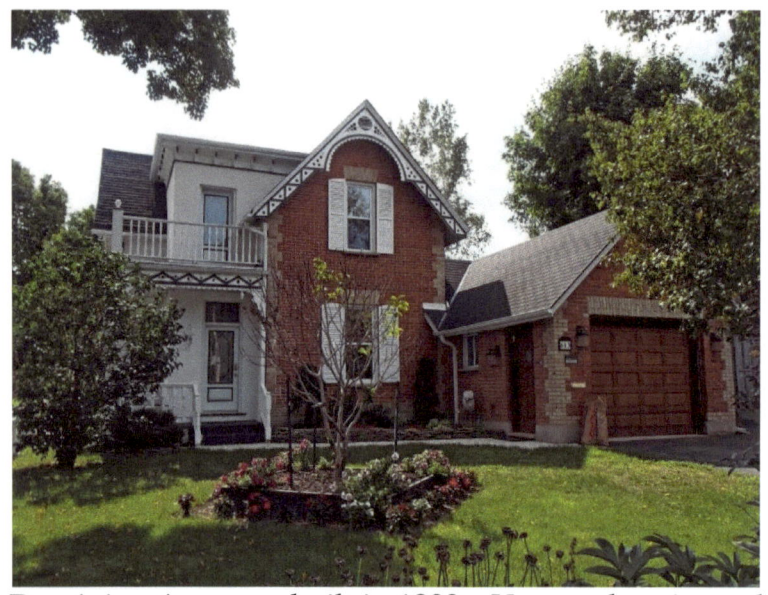

613 Dominion Avenue - built in 1900 – Vernacular - irregular layout and several different types of roofs, including flat, medium gable, and medium hipped, a decorated fascia; exterior is stretcher brick and poured concrete; upper storey balcony; windows with brick voussoirs; transom window; open platform veranda with decorated open railing and decorative trim along the roof line; wood piers to support the roof

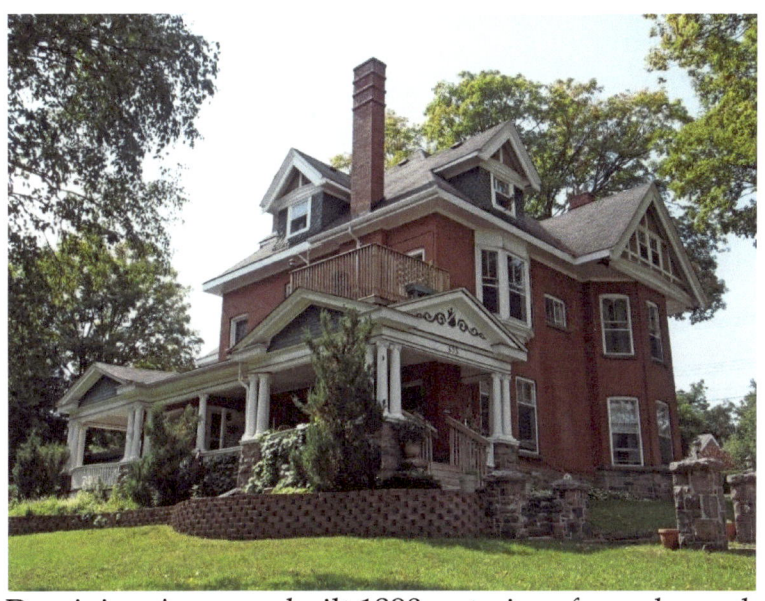

695 Dominion Avenue - built 1890, exterior of panel wood, broken course cut stone, stretcher brick, and terra cotta; medium gable roof, with decorated fascia and several gable ends with half timbering and gabled dormers; brick voussoirs; bay window on second storey; open veranda with open railing, stone, support pedestals, and Ionic capitals

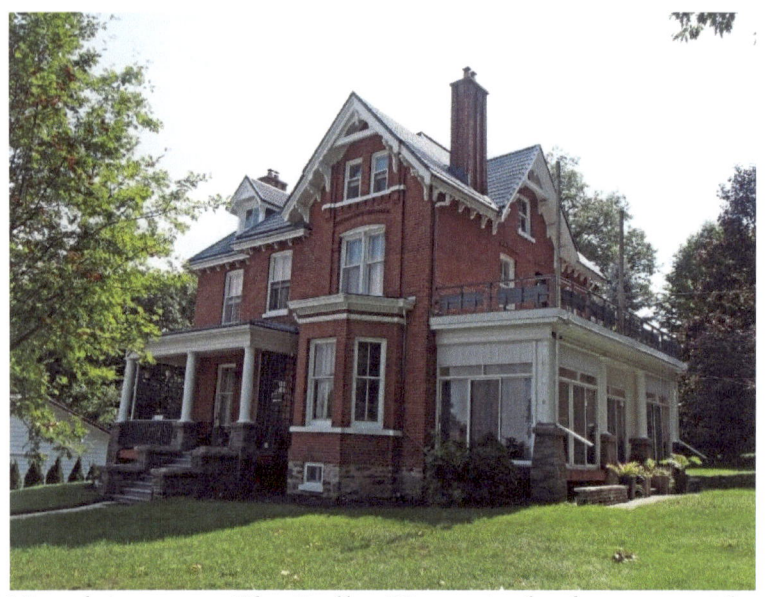

657 Hugel Avenue - The Dollar House is the former residence of two of Midland's leading historical figures: James Dollar and William Finlayson (lawyer, cabinet minister). Decorative gable ends, bracket roof trim, bay windows; medium hipped roof with several gables and gable roofed dormers; window voussoirs; two chimneys

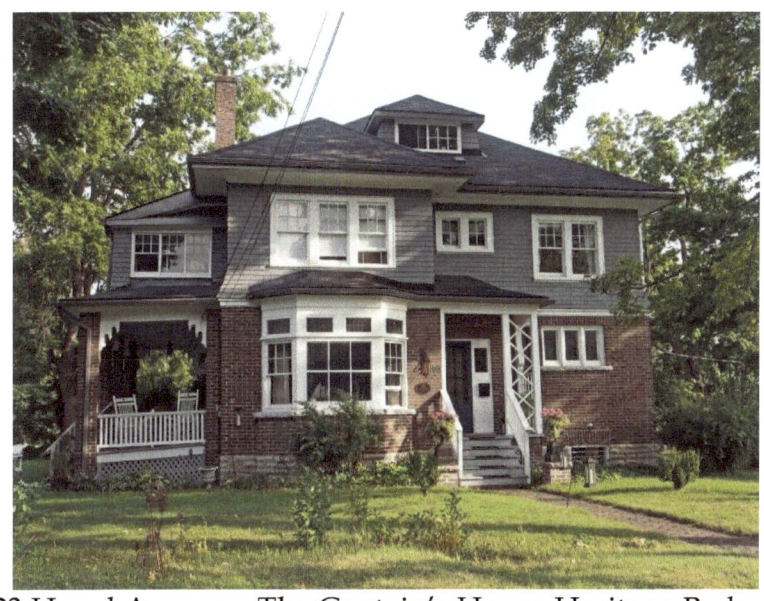

423 Hugel Avenue - The Captain's House Heritage Bed and Breakfast - built 1900 - Edwardian Classicism style, low gabled roof, siding and brick façade, numerous windows and a stone foundation; large bay window

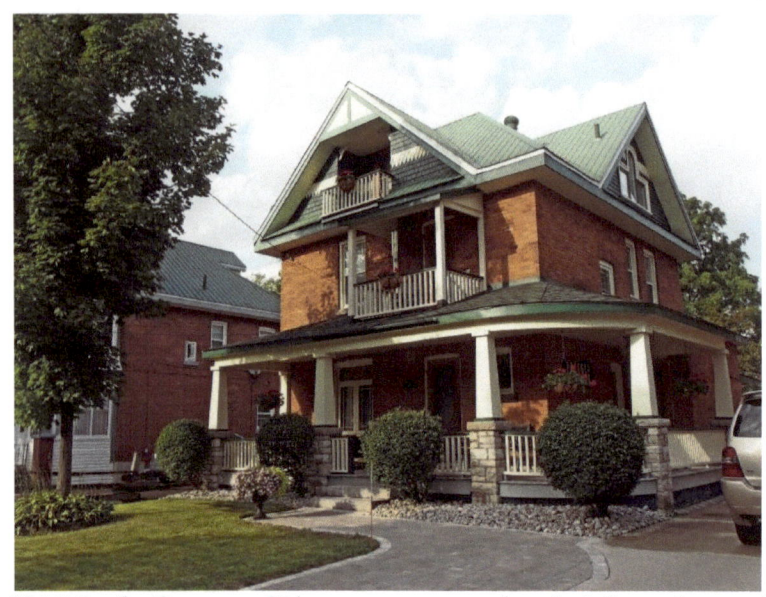

401 Manly Street – 2½ storeys; stretcher brick and wood shingle exterior; pyramidal roof with two cross gables; two balconies with open railings and decorative supports; brick voussoirs; Palladian windows in gables; wraparound veranda with stone supports, decorative piers, and open railings

Penetanguishene, Ontario – My Top 9 Picks

Penetanguishene, sometimes shortened to Penetang, is a town on the southeasterly tip of Georgian Bay. It is a bilingual, French and English, community. The name means "land of the white rolling sands".

As early as 800 A.D., the Huron settled in semi-permanent villages in the area. The young French translator, Etienne Brule, was the first European to set foot in the Penetanguishene area between 1610 and 1614.

In 1793, John Graves Simcoe, the first Lieutenant Governor of Upper Canada, visited the area and saw the location's potential as a naval base. He wanted to use the bay to shelter warships to protect British interests on lakes Huron, Erie and Michigan. Beginning in 1814, the British-Canadians built the Penetanguishene Road to provide the area a land route to Barrie and Toronto, as it was previously accessible only by water transport along the rivers or across Georgian Bay. In 1828, the main British military establishment on the Upper Lakes moved from Drummond Island to Penetanguishene. Families of Metis fur traders who had moved with the British from Michilimackinac to Drummond Island after the War of 1812, moved again to Penetanguishene. The trip from Drummond Island took from fourteen to eighteen days and the bateaux were extremely crowded as they often carried eighteen people along with provisions and household goods. Although the naval base was closed in 1834, the military base remained until 1856. Some of the troops settled in the area after their service was complete providing an English-speaking population.

In the 1840s, French-speaking families from Quebec (mainly from the area immediately east of Montreal), attracted by promises of cheap and fertile land, joined the French-speaking settlers already in the area. Later, as the logging industry began to develop, more English-speaking settlers arrived.

Alfred Andrew Thompson came to Penetanguishene in 1830 at the age of 15 to work as an assistant to Andrew Mitchell, Sr., a fur trader on Water Street. In 1840, Alfred erected a mercantile store on the corner of Water and Main Streets known as the Green Block. It was the only market in the area where farmers could sell their produce of butter, eggs, and vegetables for cash to pay their taxes. In 1847, Alfred married Sarah Anne Burke and they had three sons and two daughters. Alfred was an Anglican involved in the affairs of St. James-on-the-Line Church.

Michael Gendron, born in Quebec of French parents, came here in 1835 and established a tannery on the banks of Copeland's Creek, and later a second tannery on Main Street. "Gendron Penetangs" were a type of moccasin made of hand-stretched, oil-tanned leather, sturdy enough to be used by lumberjacks, prospectors, hunters and surveyors. They were regulation issue for soldiers in World War I.

Joseph Dubeau and his family came to the area in 1859; he started a livery stable and moved families from Penetanguishene to Midland.

The C. Beck Manufacturing Company operated from 1875 to 1969 selling wholesale lumber, shingles, lath, pails, tubs and wooden ware to firms in Ontario, Quebec, western Canada and the northern United States.

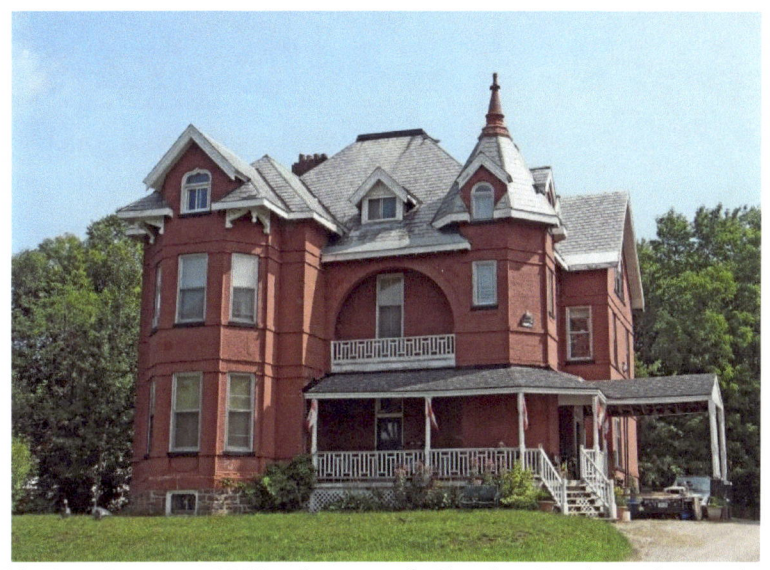

83 Fox Street – 1885 – home of Charles Beck and Amelia Dalms who had nine children (6 boys, 3 girls) – Queen Anne style – fretwork, turret, dormer, second-floor balcony, string courses wrap around the house; unique shape of window in gable

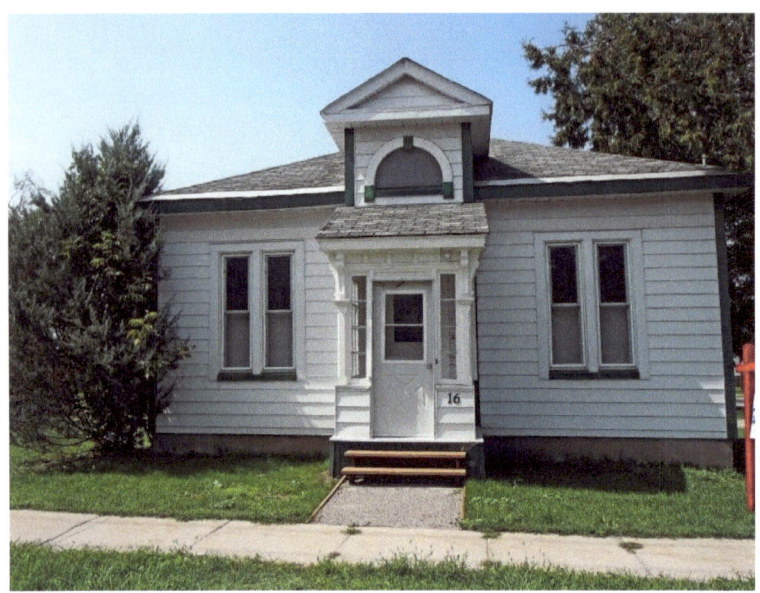

16 Peel Street – sidelights; pediment above dormer with keystone

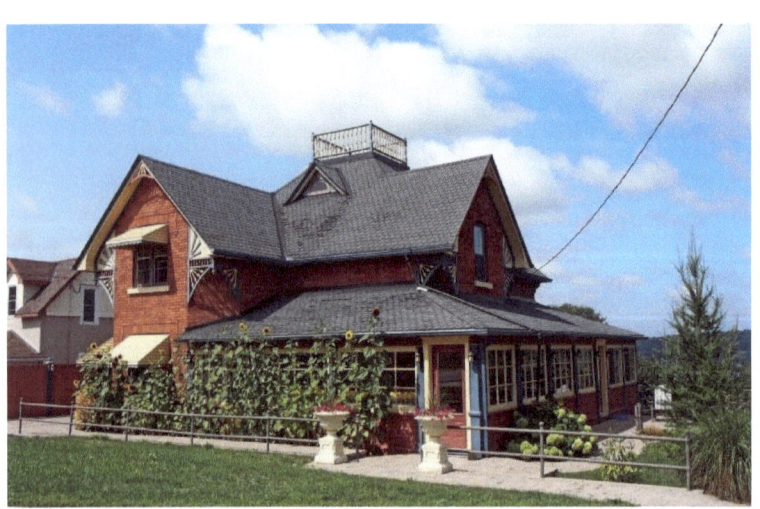

69 Poyntz Street – 1905 – built by George Pelletier, a carpenter; rooftop balcony above dormer; fretwork; enclosed wraparound veranda

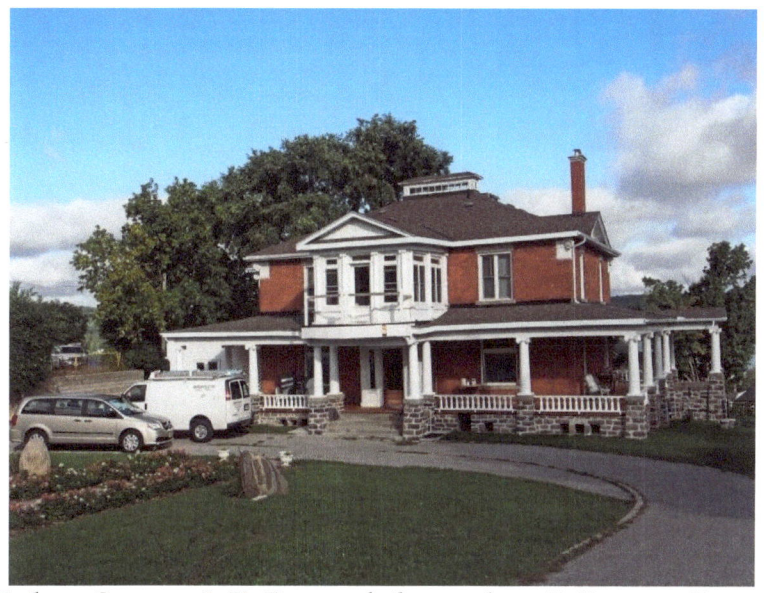

33 Robert Street – J. T. Payette's home (ran P. Payette Foundry – machine shop; built many mills)

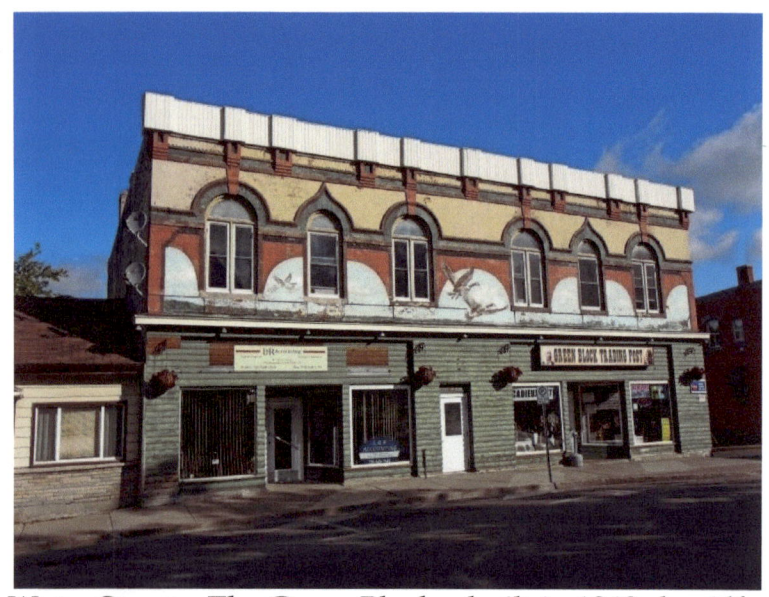

1 Water Street – The Green Block – built in 1840s by Alfred Andrew Thompson (he painted it green) for his mercantile business – now called Green Block Trading Post – voussoirs, keystones, Canada Geese mural

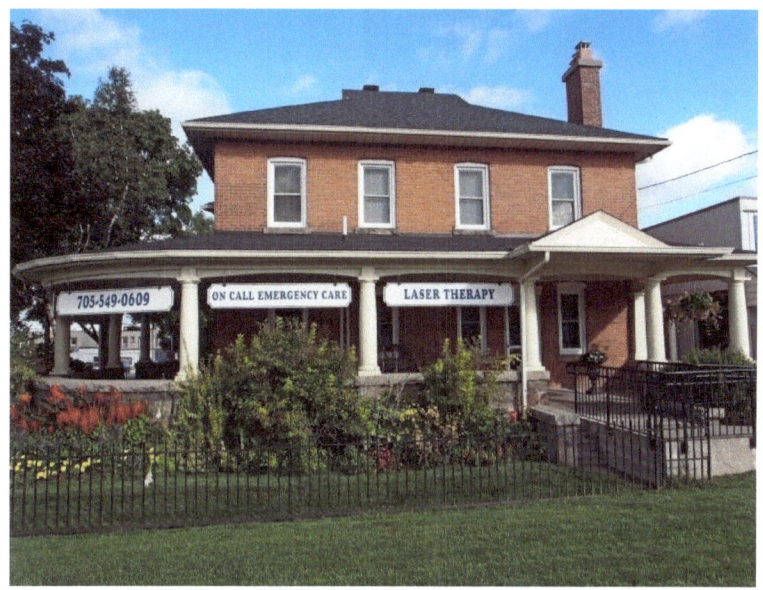

131 Main Street – home of Charles E. Wright (butcher) – 1912 - Doric pillars on wraparound verandah, pediment, hipped roof

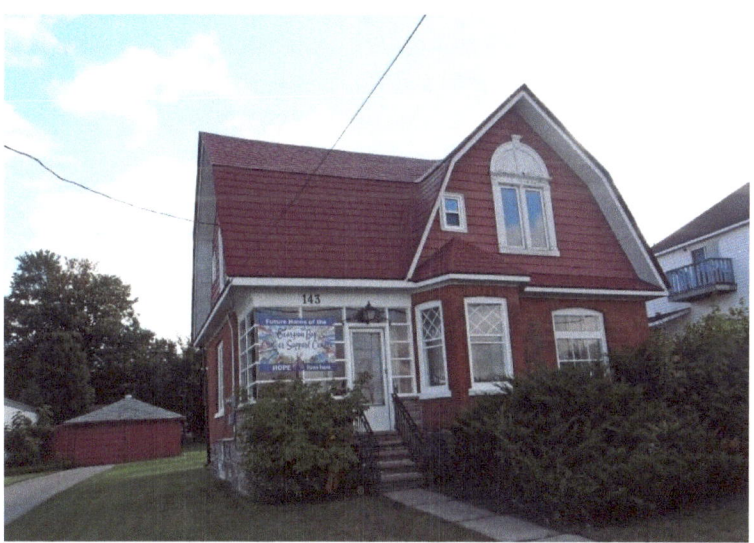

143 Main Street – Gambrel roof, Neo-colonial style

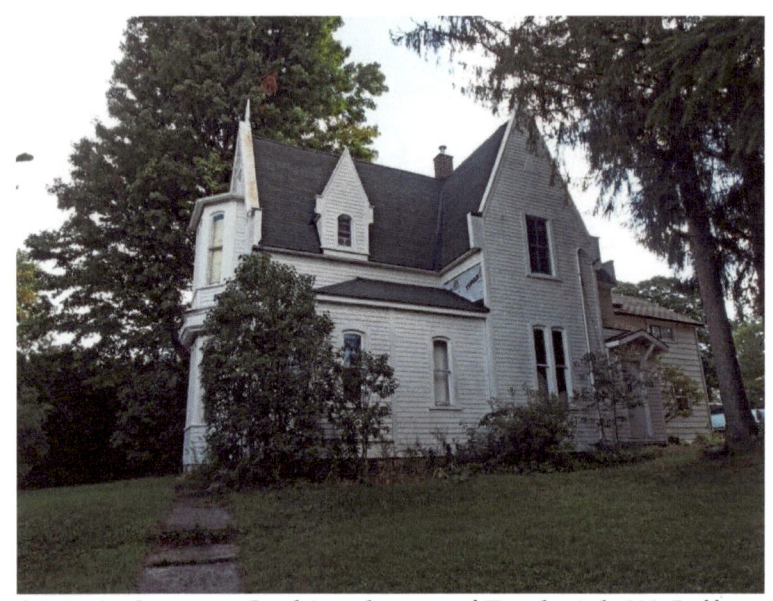

3 Maria Street – Gothic – home of Frederick W. Jeffery (bookkeeper) – 1878 – steeply pitched gable roof, verge board trim on gables, two-storey bay window, dormer

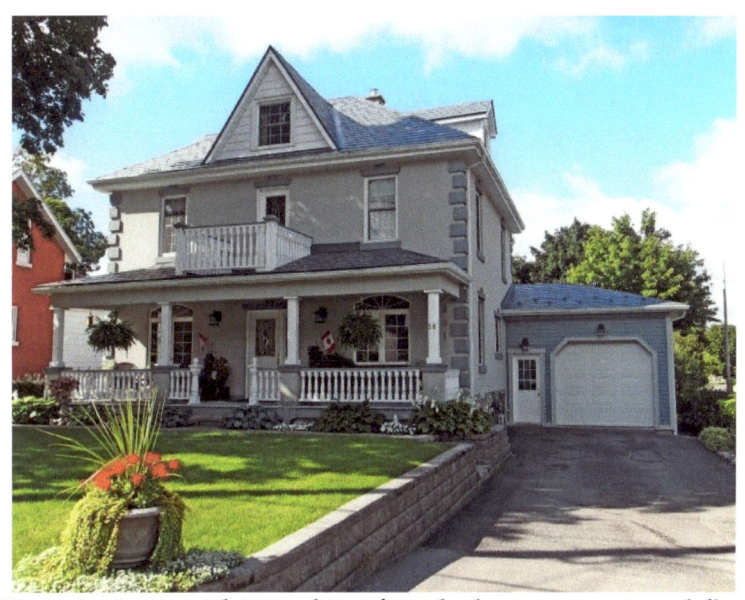

18 Maria Street – hipped roof with dormers, second floor balcony, corner quoins, multi-paned transom windows above large first storey windows, open spindle railing

Kemptville, Ontario and Area – My Top 6 Picks

Kemptville is a community located in south eastern Ontario in the northernmost part of the United Counties of Leeds and Grenville and is about fifty-six kilometres south of Ottawa. Kemptville Creek begins southwest of the town, divides Kemptville, and flows four kilometres to empty into the Rideau River. Kemptville is composed of forests and farmland. The name Kemptville was adopted in 1829 as a tribute to Sir James Kempt, the Governor of British North America.

In 1812, Lyman Clothier bought one hundred acres of land from John Byce for the price of a yoke of oxen, and a flintlock rifle. Mr. Clothier had lived in the area since 1804 or 1805, and in 1812 he and his four sons built a saw mill, and two houses in what is now Kemptville. The mill was important for the settling of the community; in order to construct a crude dwelling, lumber was required. The mill provided lumber for settlers throughout Oxford Township.

The village was located on the Ottawa-Prescott Road and many travellers passed through the settlement. One of Mr. Clothier's sons, Asa, opened his home to these travellers as a resting and meeting place. The "Clothier's Hotel" was born. A grist mill was added in 1821 when the Clothiers placed some grinding stones in the lower part of their saw mill. Rather than taking their grain to a site on the St. Lawrence River, a daunting hike in the best of conditions, the settlers could now take it to this grist mill. A blacksmith's shop was built and run by the Clothiers. A schoolhouse was built in 1823 and served the surrounding communities for many years. The first doctor arrived in the community in 1824. A weekly newspaper is published in Kemptville, called the *Kemptville Advance*, and has been published since 1855.

Elizabethtown-Kitley is a township in eastern Ontario in the United Counties of Leeds and Grenville. Its southern border lies along the St. Lawrence River and it extends north into many rural hamlets and villages. Also in the township are Addison, Forthton, and Newbliss.

Newbliss was settled mostly by Loyalists or immigrants from the British Isles who received their land here as grants from the Crown. One of the first businesses to operate here was Dack's Tavern, built in 1817 and established as a tavern around the 1830s. The tavern had five rooms, three bed and horse stables, and also hosted Orange Lodge meetings. By the mid-1800s, the village began to flourish when roads improved in the area. By this time, the settlement consisted of two hotels, a blacksmith shop, a wagon shop, a general store, a post office, and its own schoolhouse. A cheese factory consisting of three buildings operated from Newbliss. The main building was later turned into the general store.

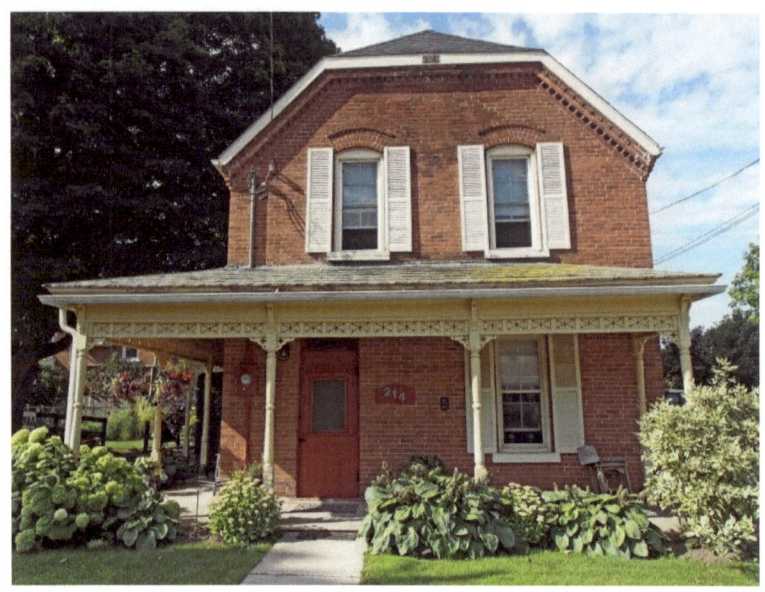

214 Prescott Street – 1897 – decorative brickwork under cornice; open wooden veranda with decorative railings and support posts

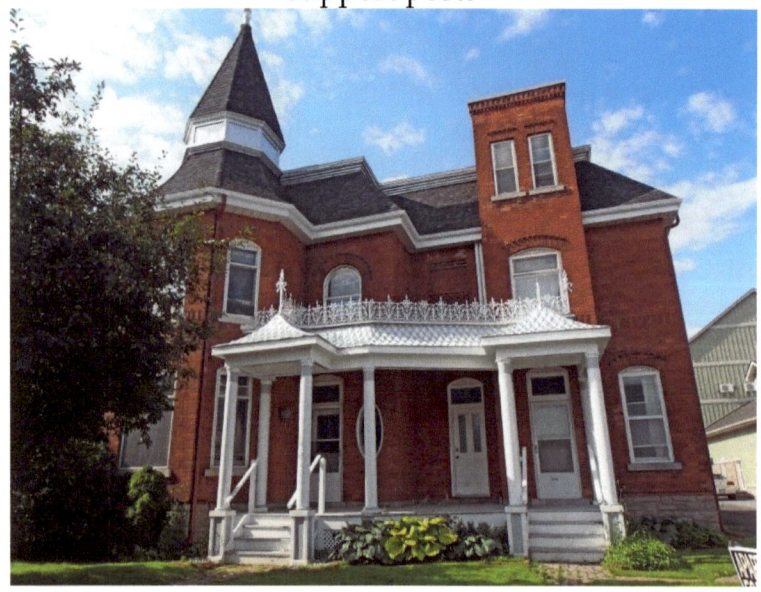

220-222 Prescott Street – de Pencier House – 1897- brick – Queen Anne style – tower, turret, iron cresting

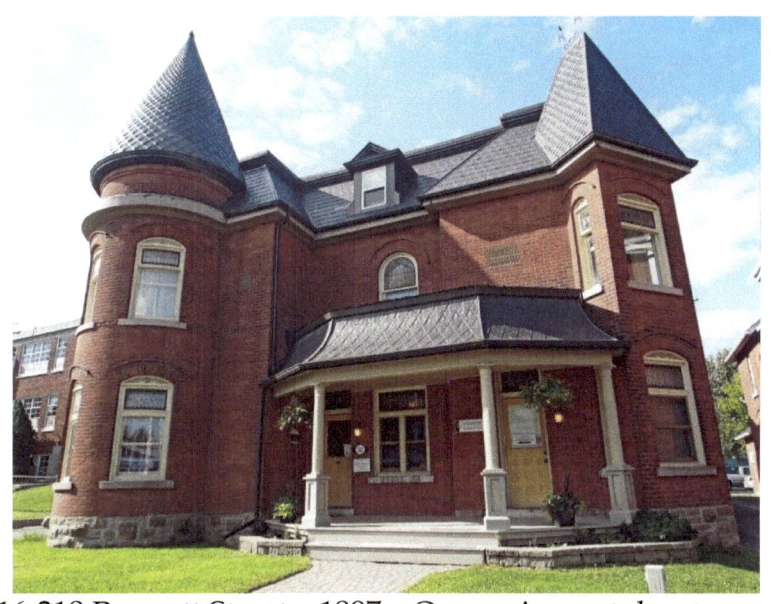

216-218 Prescott Street – 1897 – Queen Anne style – towers, dormer

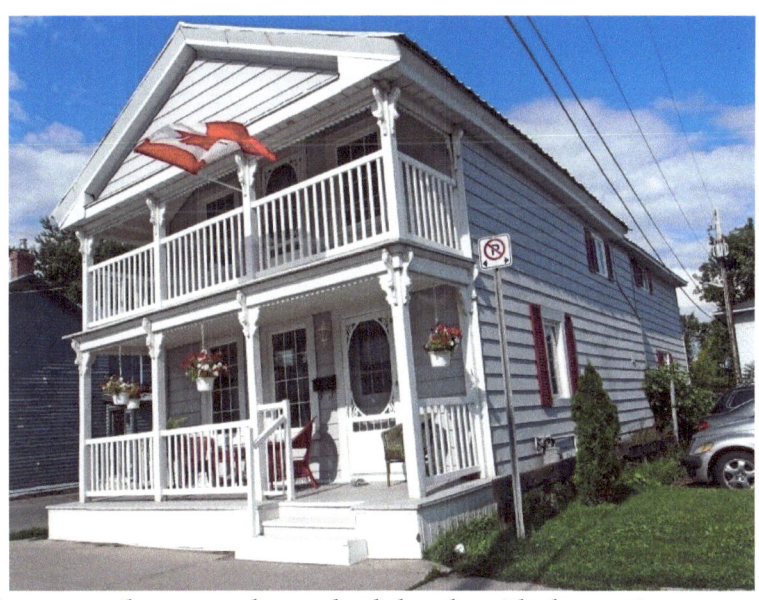

Open wooden verandas on both levels with decorative support posts and open railings

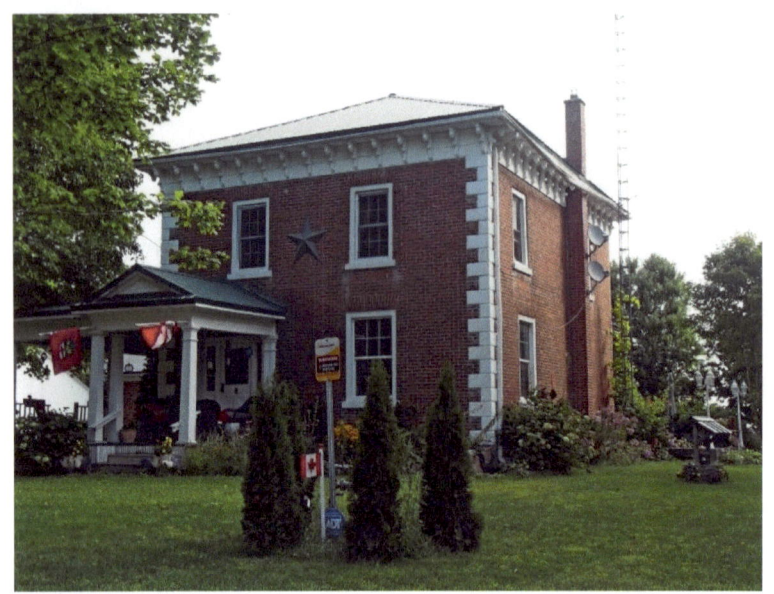

Addison - Hipped roof, cornice brackets, corner quoins, pediment

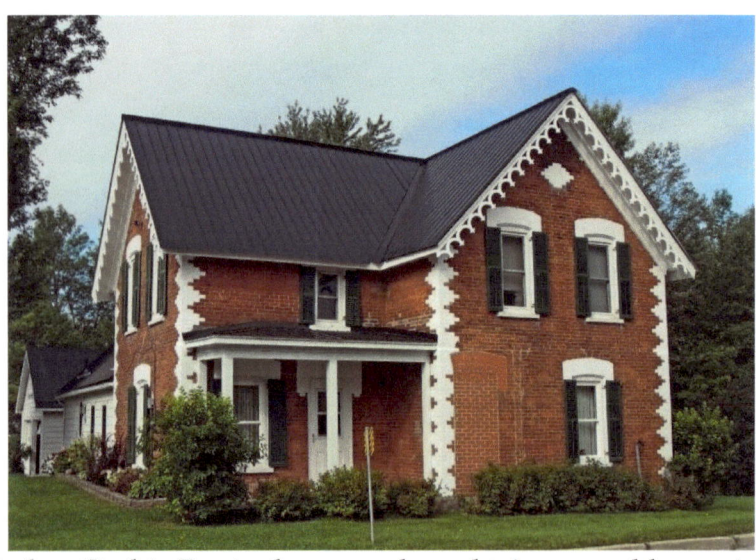

Toledo - Gothic Revival – verge board trim on gables, painted corner quoins and voussoirs

Cornwall, Ontario – My Top 9 Picks

Cornwall is Ontario's easternmost city, located on the Saint Lawrence River about one hundred kilometres southeast of Ottawa. It is named after the English Duchy of Cornwall.

In June 1784, disbanded Loyalist soldiers and their families settled at New Johnstown, the site of present day Cornwall. Native traders and French missionaries and explorers came here in the 17th and early 18th centuries. By 1805 Cornwall had a court house, a schoolhouse, two churches and many homes. The construction of the Cornwall Canal in 1834-42 accelerated its development. Mills and large factories were erected along the canal.

The Cornwall Canal, a series of locks which carried boats 18.5 kilometers around the rapids, was used for over one hundred years. Power drawn from the canal attracted textile and paper mills. The textile industry played a major role in Cornwall's economic and cultural development. This canal was one of eight canals that connected western Canada with the ocean by way of the Great Lakes and the St. Lawrence River. The Canal was an important shipping center until the completion of The St. Lawrence Seaway in 1959.

Eastern Ontario has always been a highway or corridor through which people moved, a corridor used by migration and conquest. Prior to European colonization, the Mohawks and Six Nations Iroquois settled and raided through the St. Lawrence valley. The French and British fought over the waterway and, after the American Revolution in 1812–14, it became a battleground between Americans and Canadians. Formally founded to be a new home for refugees, it remained a home for refugees and migrants for much of its history.

Slavery was ended in the colony of Upper Canada in stages, beginning in 1793 when importing slaves was banned, and culminating in 1819 when Upper Canada Attorney-General John Robinson declared all slaves in the colony to be freed, making Upper Canada the first place in the British Empire to unequivocally move towards abolition.

The aftermath of the American Revolution resulted in the formal division of Upper and Lower Canada (later Ontario and Quebec) to accommodate Loyalists fleeing persecution in the new United States, and distribution of land throughout Southern Ontario brought major change to Eastern Ontario.

The original 516 settlers arrived with minimal supplies and faced years of hard work and possible starvation. Upon their departure from military camps in Montreal, Pointe Claire, Saint Anne, and Lachine in the fall of 1784, Loyalists were given a tent, one month's worth of food rations, clothes, and agricultural provisions by regiment commanders. They were promised one cow for every two families, an axe, and other necessary tools in the near future. For the next three years, bateaux (boat) crews delivered rations to the township, after which residents were left to fend for themselves.

Cornwall was unusually integrated for a town in Ontario. For hundreds of years, the local population has been characterized by a mix of economic migrants, refugees and opportunists. Mixing of different social classes and ethnic backgrounds was common even early in its history, due to the interdependence demanded by isolation and the lack of support or interference from authorities.

In the 1780s to1830s, a "Bee" was a social event that pooled local labor resources, and was often a festive occasion. These "Bees" drew on many different classes, backgrounds and ethnic and linguistic groups working together for survival. These were very common in Eastern Ontario generally, and especially so in the early villages of the St. Lawrence valley.

Cornwall was once home to a thriving cotton processing industry. Courtaulds Canada, Inc.'s rayon manufacturing mill operated until 1992. Domtar, a Quebec-based company, operated a paper mill in the city for nearly 100 years, ceasing operations in 2006. Cornwall's industrial base has now shifted to a more diversified mix of manufacturing, automotive, high tech, food processing, distribution centers and call centers.

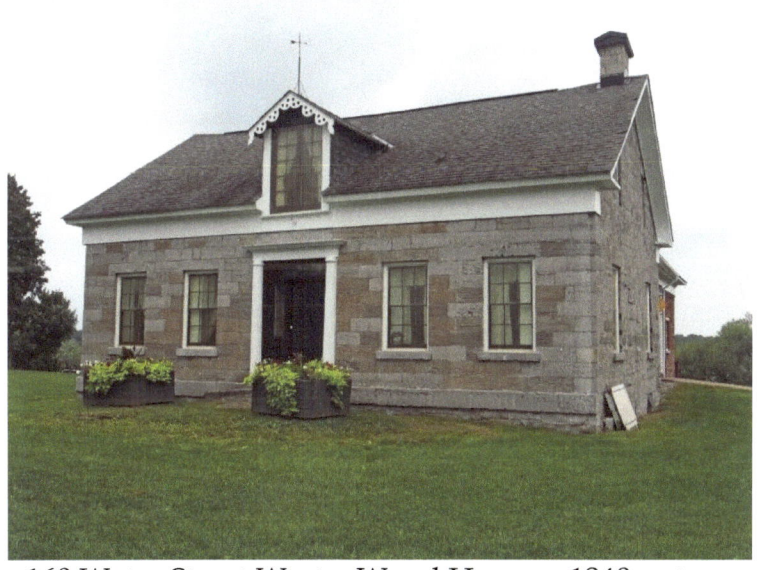

160 Water Street West – Wood House – 1840 – stone homestead – now Cornwall Community Museum

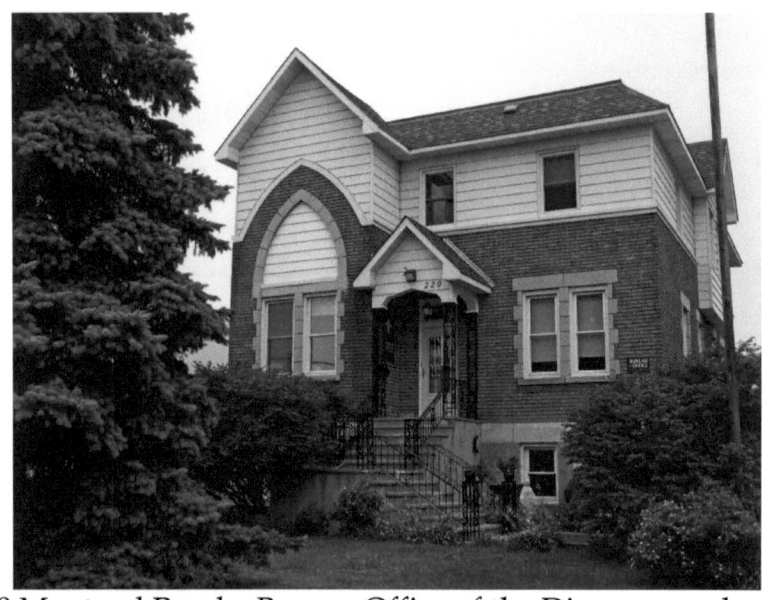

220 Montreal Road – Bureau Office of the Diocese – arch over window with blind tympanum, open pediment above door

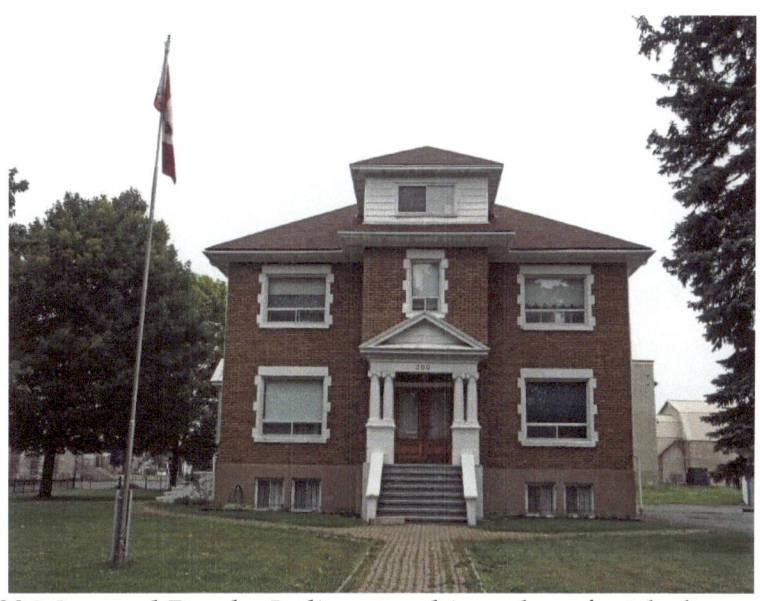

300 Montreal Road – Italianate – hipped roof with dormer; pillars with Ionic capitals; pediment; quoining around windows

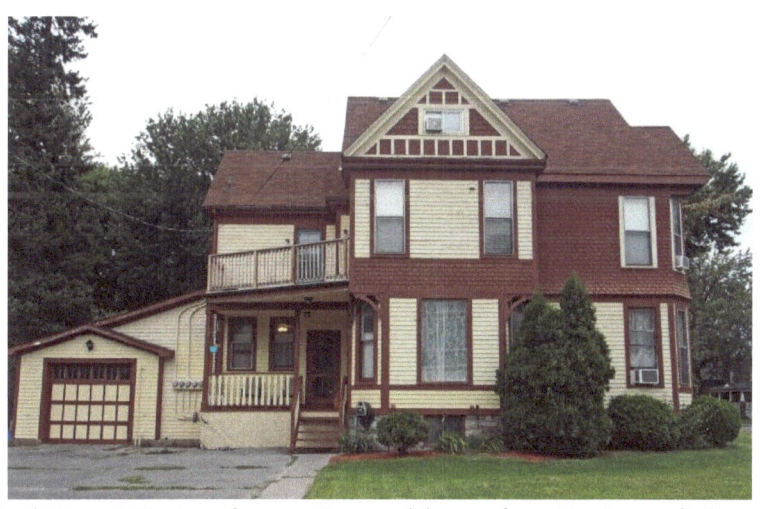

Third Street East – decorative gable on frontispiece, fish scale patterning, fretwork; second floor balcony

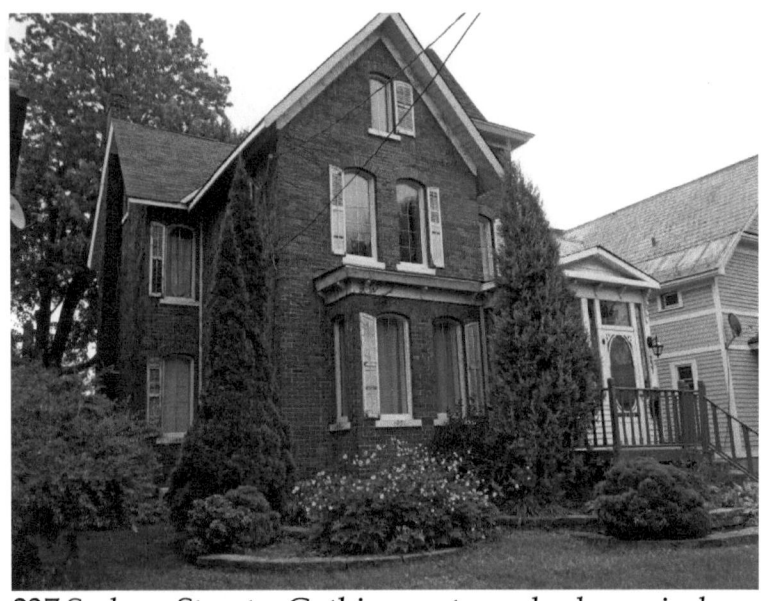

237 Sydney Street – Gothic – rectangular bay window; enclosed porch with cornice brackets and pediment

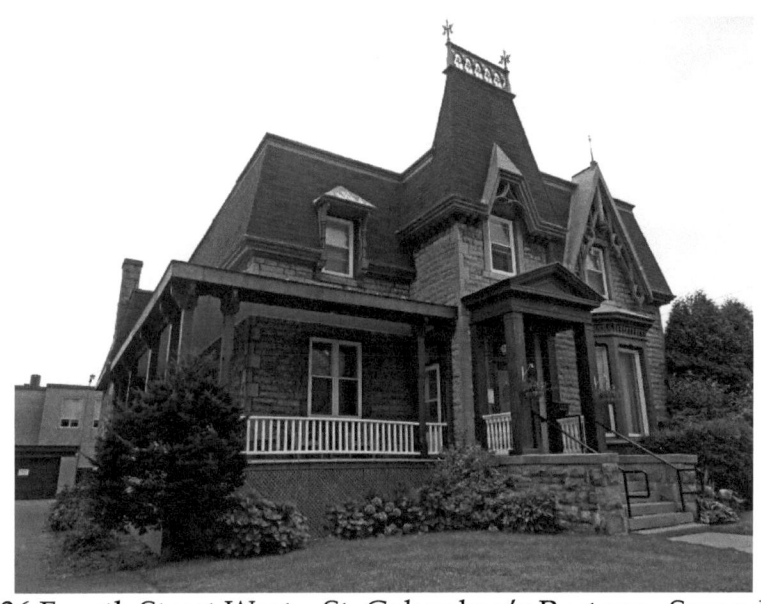

36 Fourth Street West – St. Columban's Rectory - Second Empire domestic architecture with mansard roof and detailing; window hood, trim on gable, bay window, cornice brackets; open railing on porch and wraparound verandah

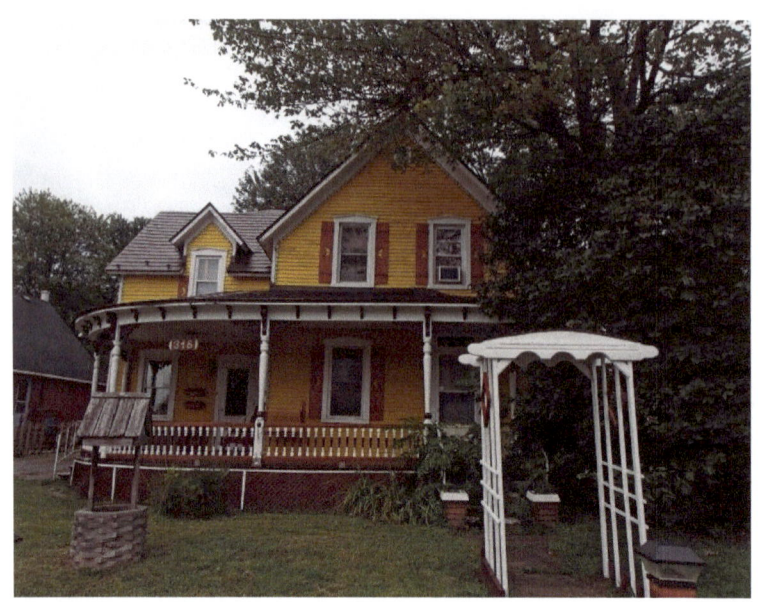

318 Augustus Street – Gothic Revival – wraparound verandah with cornice brackets, turned spindle supports, and open spindle railing

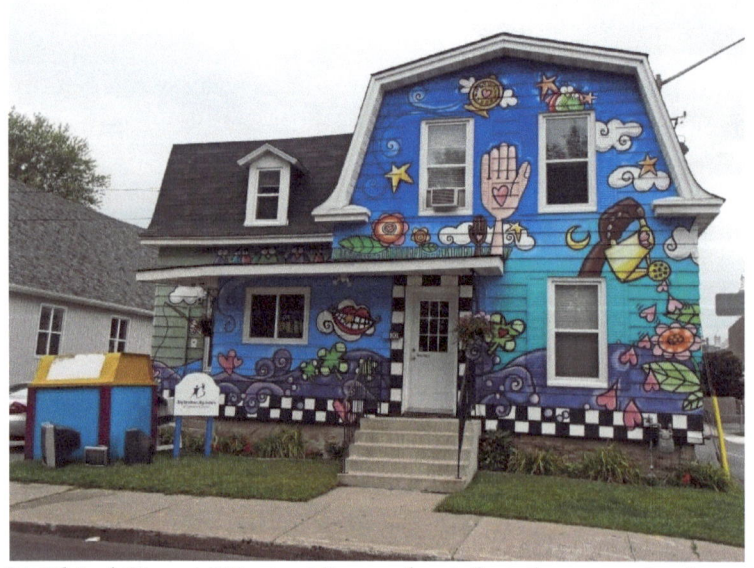

101 Third Street West – Neo-colonial style – gambrel roof, dormer

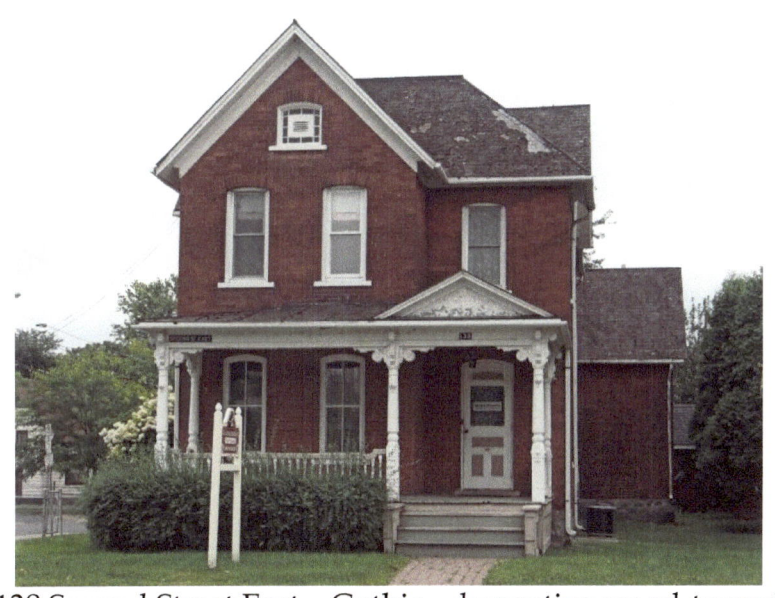

138 Second Street East – Gothic - decorative wood-turned veranda support posts, open railing, pediment with decorative tympanum

www.ingramcontent.com/pod-product-compliance
Lightning Source LLC
Chambersburg PA
CBHW040225220526
45473CB00001B/130